ON THIS DAY
in BLACK HISTORY

BUSHEL & PECK BOOKS

Text copyright © 2021 by Judy Johnson and Vicki DeFendis

Published by Bushel & Peck Books, www.bushelandpeckbooks.com.

Bushel & Peck Books is dedicated to fighting illiteracy all over the world. For every book we sell, we donate one to a child in need—book for book. To nominate a school or organization to receive free books, please visit www.bushelandpeckbooks.com.

Type set in Josefin Sans, Prater Script Pro, Cheap Pine Sans, and Scrapbook Basic.

LCCN: TK
ISBN: 9781638191391

First Edition

Printed in the United States

10 9 8 7 6 5 4 3 2 1

Judy Johnson and Vicki DeFendis

ON THIS DAY

in
BLACK
HISTORY

A KID'S
DAY-BY-DAY
GUIDE TO
SIGNIFICANT
EVENTS

INTRODUCTION

Dear Reader,

You may find that some of the facts included in this book spark questions and pique your curiosity. That's good! Do your own research and find out what you can about a topic or person that you find interesting. Notice the year of the events as you read them. Many of the accomplishments mentioned here are not remarkable when compared with today's culture and events, but when you look at them in the context of the time they were achieved, they can be thought of as nothing short of miraculous, or well overdue. This is by no means a complete and finite list of the events and achievements of Blacks in history in the United States or the world. There are many important and interesting facts that are not included. That, dear reader, is your job—to find them and make sure they are not forgotten. This is just a place to start.

—Judy and Vicki

📑 JANUARY 1

1804 The Haitian Independence Act declares Haiti free from France.

1808 The "Act Prohibiting the Importation of Slaves" makes it illegal to transport slaves from other nations.

1808 The African Benevolent Society for Education is founded to finance free schools for Blacks.

1863 The Emancipation Proclamation goes into effect, freeing all American slaves.

1923 The foremost jazz vibraphone player in history, African American Milt Jackson, is born in Detroit, Michigan. Jackson recorded with many jazz greats, including, Miles Davis, Thelonious Monk, John Coltrane, and Oscar Peterson.

A stamp printed in France shows Miles Dewey Davis III

JANUARY 2

1831 *The Liberator*, an abolitionist newspaper, is started by white publisher William Lloyd Garrison in Boston, Massachusetts. Garrison includes his American Anti-Slavery Society Declaration of Sentiments calling for Congress to restrict the slave trade and abolish slavery in U. S. territories and boycotting cotton and slave produced goods.

1898 Influential Black lawyer and activist, Sadie Alexander is born in Philadelphia, Pennsylvania. She was the first woman to be elected to any office of the National Bar Association.

1906 Esquire Magazine illustrator and cartoonist, African American Elmer Campbell, is born in St. Louis, Missouri.

1913 Juanita Mitchell, social activist, and the first African American woman to be admitted to the Maryland Bar, is born in Hot Springs, Arkansas.

1915 African American historian, and author John Hope Franklin is born in Rentiesville, Oklahoma. Franklin received the Presidential Medal of Freedom from Pres. Bill Clinton in 1995.

1965 A nationwide protest movement begins with a voter drive in Selma, Alabama by the Sothern Christian Leadership Conference.

FEB
MAR
APR
MAY
JUN
JUL
AUG
SEP
OCT
NOV
DEC

JAN

 # JANUARY 3

1624 William Tucker, the first black child born in America, is baptized.

1793 White Quaker abolitionist and preacher, Lucretia Coffin Mott, is born in Nantucket, Massachusetts.

1834 South Carolina's first African American lieutenant governor, politician, and integrationist, Alonzo Jacob Ransier is born as a freeman in Charleston, South Carolina.

1941 Franklin McCain, one of the four African Americans who initiated sit-ins at lunch counters throughout the south, is born in Union County, North Carolina. McCain remained active in civil rights for the rest of his life.

1958 Black politician, President of the National Urban League, and civic advocate, Marc Morial is born in New Orleans, Louisiana. Both Marc Morial and his father, Ernest Morial, served as mayor of New Orleans.

1968 Popular African American actor of the 1990s and 2000's, Cuba Gooding, Jr., is born in the Bronx, New York. Gooding won an Academy Award in 1996 for his role in the move *Jerry Maguire*.

1969 The first African American woman elected to Congress, Shirley Chisholm begins her long and illustrious career in politics.

JANUARY 4

1872 African American education advocate and one of the founders of the National Parent Teachers Association (PTA), Selena Butler is born in Thomasville, Georgia.

1908 Gifted African American mathematician William Claytor is born in Norfolk, Virginia.

1911 Actor, musician, and all-around entertainer, Slim Gaillard, is born in Detroit, Michigan.

1920 The National Negro Baseball League is organized.

1935 Olympic gold medal boxer and Heavyweight Champion, African American Floyd Patterson is born in Waco, North Carolina.

2003 The Indianapolis Colts and the New York Jets square off in the National Football League (NFL) playoffs. This is the first time two Black NFL coaches, the Colts' Tony Dungy, and the Jets' Herman Edwards, meet in the playoffs.

JANUARY 5

1804 "Black Laws" are passed in Ohio that limit the legal rights of free blacks.

JAN

1893 African American inventive and pioneering self-taught folk guitarist Elizabeth Cotton is born in Chapel Hill, North Carolina. Cotton was over 60 when she began performing due to a fluke meeting with the famous folk music family, the Seeger's.

1926 Civil rights activist, politician and member of the Southern Christian Leadership Conference, African American Hosea Williams is born in Attapulgus, Georgia.

1931 Noted and respected choreographer of African American dance, Alvin Ailey was born in Rogers, Texas.

1935 Unrelenting African American baseball catcher, coach, and teacher Earl Battey is born in Los Angeles, California.

1943 Scientist, botanist, and inventor of George Washington Carver dies in Tuskegee, Alabama.

"BLOODY SUNDAY", MARCH 7, 1965

He Fed the Hungry

"UNBOSSED AND UNBOUGHT"

Monument honoring the Reverend Hosea Williams, Sr.

JANUARY 6

1811 Steadfast white abolitionist and politician, Charles Sumner, is born in Boston, Massachusetts.

1916 Ambassador, economist, teacher, and Cornell's first Black football player, Jerome Holland is born in Auburn, New York.

1948 The Women's Army Corps (WAC) becomes integrated.

2004 The family of Amadou Diallo receives $3million from the City of New York for their wrongful death suit. Diallo was shot and killed by police in 1999 while unarmed.

2005 Edgar Ray Killen is charged with the murders of three civil rights workers; Andrew Goodman, James Chaney, and Michael Schwerner, who were found dead in their burned-out car in June 1964. Killen is sentenced to 60 years in prison for his participation in the killings.

JANUARY 7

1890 African American W.B. Pervis patents the fountain pen.

1891 Known best for her novel *Their Eyes were Watching God*, African American writer Zora Neale

JAN
FEB
MAR
APR
MAY
JUN
JUL
AUG
SEP
OCT
NOV
DEC

Hurston is born in Notasulga, Alabama.

1927 The first game by the predominantly Black team the Harlem Globetrotters is played in Hinckley Illinois.

1955 Marian Anderson is the first Black person to have a leading role in the Metropolitan Opera of New York.

1985 Record-setting Black British Formula One race car driver and social activist, Lewis Hamilton is born in Stevenage, Hertfordshire, England.

2002 The first African American mayor of Atlanta, Shirley Clarke Franklin, is inaugurated.

JANUARY 8

1811 The German Coast Uprising, a revolt of almost 150 slaves near New Orleans, Louisiana, begins.

1865 Former slave Fannie M. Jackson is the first American born black women to graduate from a major college (Oberlin College).

1911 Best known for her portrayal of Scarlett O'Hara's servant girl, Prissy, in *Gone with the Wind*, Theresa "Butterfly" McQueen is born in Tampa, Florida. McQueen was unable to attend the premiere of the movie because it was shown in a segregated theater.

1912 W. E. B. DuBois helps to establish the African National Congress in South Africa to address the issues facing Black Africans.

1940 Founder of Blackside Productions, producer and filmmaker, Henry Hampton, is born in St. Louis, Missouri.

1956 Jackie Robinson is awarded the Spingarn medal by the National Association for the Advancement of Colored People (NAACP) for his for his support and leadership on civil rights issues.

2007 The first woman African American to graduate from Yale Law School and first female Black judge in the U. S., Jane Matilda Bolin, dies at the age of 98 in Long Island City, New York.

JANUARY 9

1849 The son of a Black Seminole Chief, U. S. Army scout, and recipient of the Congressional Medal of Honor, Pompey Factor, is born in Arkansas.

1866 The Fisk School for Freedmen, now known as Fisk University, holds its first classes in Nashville, Tennessee. Fisk is an HBCU.

1869 Baltimore School #1 is opened. The school evolves into the Baltimore Normal School for Colored Teachers, and eventually into Bowie

JAN
FEB
MAR
APR
MAY
JUN
JUL
AUG
SEP
OCT
NOV
DEC

State University (BSU) in Bowie, Maryland. BSU is an HBCU.

1914 Innovative jazz drummer and bandleader, African American Kenny Clarke, is born in Pittsburgh, Pennsylvania.

1935 African American Earl Graves, Sr., publisher of Black Enterprise Magazine, is born in White Plains, New York.

1937 Epic author, journalist, and administrator, African American Leon Richard Forrest, is born in Chicago, Illinois.

 # JANUARY 10

1750 The first bishop of the African Methodist Episcopal Zion Church, James Varick, is born near Newburgh, New York.

1915 Distinguished African American orchestral conductor, Dean Dixon, is born in New York, New York.

1916 International African American artist and print maker, Eldzier Cortor is born in Richmond, Virginia.

1936 African American activist for racial desegregation, Thelma Joyce White, is born in Marlin, Texas.

1957 The Southern Leadership Conference is founded with Martin Luther King, Jr. as president.

1967 The first elected African American U. S. Senator from Massachusetts, Edward Brooke, takes office.

 # JANUARY 11

1879 After an ultimatum issued by the British Army to the Zulu, the British invade Zululand in a 6-month war, ending in the slaughter of many Zulu warriors.

1961 Charlotte Hawkins Brown, founder of the Palmer Memorial Institute, an African American Boarding School, dies in Greensboro, North Carolina.

1965 Unable to receive basic accommodations in New Orleans Louisiana, Black AFL All-Star players from the Buffalo Bills boycott the game. The game is moved to Houston, Texas.

1971 Distinctive African American singer and actress Mary J. Blige is born in Savannah, Georgia.

 # JANUARY 12

1848 George B. Vashon is the first African American to be admitted to the New York Bar Association.

1890 Educational leader and first African American president of Howard University, Mordecai Johnson is born in Paris, Tennessee. Johnson aggressively fought for and raised money to improve the school.

1920 Co-founder of The Committee for Racial Equity (latter called Congress for Racial Equity), African American James Farmer, Jr. is born in Marshall, Texas.

1950 Lawyer, congresswoman, and member of the Congressional Black Caucus Sheila Jackson Lee is born in Queens, New York.

1959 What becomes the largest African American music label in the U. S., Motown records is established by Berry Gordy, Jr.

1971 The Congressional Black Caucus is organized to help address the concerns of African Americans.

 # JANUARY 13

1808 White member of the Anti-slavery Society and lawyer for many runaway slaves, Salmon chase is born in New Hampshire.

1850 The first African American woman lawyer in the United States and first woman to be admitted to the Washington, D. C. Bar Association, Charlotte Ray is born in New York, New York.

1905 The lead singer for Duke Ellington's band for many years, African American Ivie Anderson is born in Gilroy, California.

1913 Jarvis Christian Institute, a school for Black youth, and later to become Jarvis Christian College (JCC) opens its doors to students in Hawkins, Texas. JCC is an HBCU.

1990 L. Douglas Wilder becomes the first African American Governor of Virginia since reconstruction.

 # JANUARY 14

1914 Publisher, poet, and librarian, African American Dudley Randall is born in Washington, D. C.

1916 African American novelist and founder of the Harlem Writers Guild, John Oliver Killens is born in Macon, Georgia.

1937 Allen Toussaint is born in New Orleans, Louisiana. He was an African American musician, composer, and music producer.

1940 African American civil rights activist, and politician Julian Bond is born in Nashville, Tennessee. Bond helped to establish the SNCC.

1945 Black movie and TV actress of the 1970s Lawrence Vonetta McGee is born in San Francisco, California.

1969 The University of Minnesota's administration building is taken

JAN
FEB
MAR
APR
MAY
JUN
JUL
AUG
SEP
OCT
NOV
DEC

over by African American student protestors demanding educational and social considerations.

 # JANUARY 15

1888 Doctor and surgeon Austin Curtis is born in Raleigh, North Carolina. Curtis was the first African American attending doctor at an all-white hospital.

1929 Center of the American Civil Rights Movement and recipient of the Nobel Peace Prize, Martin Luther King, Jr. is born in Atlanta, Georgia.

1933 African American novelist and author of *The Autobiography of Miss Jane Pittman*, Ernest Gaines is born on River Lake Plantation in Louisiana.

1936 The Maryland Supreme Court rules in Murry v. Pearson that the University of Maryland must include African Americans. This is one of African American Superior Court judge Thurgood Marshall's first court cases.

1991 Roland Burris becomes Illinois' first Black attorney general.

1998 African American civil rights activist James Farmer receives the Medal of Freedom by President Bill Clinton.

JANUARY 16

1871 Notable historian of Africa and African Americans and advocate of art, Charles Seifert is born in Barbados.

1943 Recipient of the Bronze Star and the first female African American U. S. Air Force General, Marcelite Jordan Harris is born in Houston, Texas.

1950 African American dancer, actor, and director Debbie Allen is born in Houston, Texas.

1967 Lucius Amerson is sworn in as sheriff of Macon County, Georgia, the first black sheriff in the South since Reconstruction.

1979 Native American and African American singer and actor Aaliyah Haughton is born in Brooklyn, New York. Her life was tragically cut short in a plane crash at the age of 22.

1986 The first bust of a Black American, Martin Luther King, Jr. is displayed in the halls of Congress.

 # JANUARY 17

1759 Black nationalist, Ship builder, and captain Paul Cuffee is born in Cuttyjunk, Massachusetts.

JAN
FEB
MAR
APR
MAY
JUN
JUL
AUG
SEP
OCT
NOV
DEC

1881 HBCU Tillotson Collegiate and Normal Institute, now Huston-Tillotson University, opens its doors to its first 250 students.

1899 African American economic activist and analysist Abram Lincoln Harris, Jr. is born in Richmond, Virginia.

1928 Singular international entertainer Eartha Kitt is born in South Carolina.

1931 Distinguished actor and narrator, James Earl Jones is born in Arkabulta, Mississippi. Jones is known for being the voice of Darth Vader in the Star Wars movies and Mufasa in *The Lion King*.

1942 Three-time World Heavyweight Boxing Champion and activist, Muhammad Ali (birth name Cassius Clay) is born in Louisville, Kentucky.

 # JANUARY 18

1856 African American and the first surgeon to successfully perform open heart surgery, Dr. Daniel H. William, is born in Hollidaysburg, Pennsylvania.

1949 William L. Dawson becomes the first African American to be chairman of a Congressional Committee.

1958 The first Black to player in the National Hockey

League game is Willie O'Ree. O'Ree played professional hockey for almost 20 years.

1966 The first Black presidential cabinet member, Robert C. Weaver, is sworn in as the Secretary of Housing.

1998 Dr. Martin Luther King, Jr. Day observed as a holiday for the first time by the New York Stock Exchange.

 ## JANUARY 19

1898 African American George Dawson is born in Marshall, Texas. Marshal learned to read and write at 98 years old. He wrote and published a book, *Life is So Good*, at 102 years old.

1906 Urban League administrator and activist Anna Tanneyhill is born in Boston, Massachusetts.

1918 Publisher and the first African American to be included in *Forbes* "400 Richest Americans," John Johnson is born in Arkansas City, Arkansas.

1931 The first African American Master Diver in the U. S. Navy, Car Brashear is born in Tonieville, Kentucky.

FEB
MAR
APR
MAY
JUN
JUL
AUG
SEP
OCT
NOV
DEC

JANUARY 20

1847 The founder of the Alabama Penny Savings Bank, a bank for African Americans, W. R. Pettiford is born.

1895 Educator, singer, and choral director, African American Eva Jessye is born in Coffeyville, Kansas.

1903 African American lawyer, judge and civil rights activist Loren Miller is born in Pender, Nebraska.

1986 The first observance of Martin Luther King, Jr. Day as a national holiday.

2001 The first African American U. S. Secretary of Education, Rod Paige, is confirmed by the Senate.

2009 The first African American President of the United States of America Barack Obama, is sworn in.

JANUARY 21

1813 White explorer, stalwart abolitionist, and politician John C. Fremont is born in Savannah, Georgia.

1906 The first African American officer in the Civil Air Patrol and civil rights activist, Willa Brown is born in Glasgow, Kentucky.

1941 Folk singer and songwriter Richie Havens is born in Brooklyn. New York. Havens is most noted for being the opening act for the original Woodstock concert in 1969.

1951 The first African American Attorney General of the United States Eric Holder is born in The Bronx, New York.

2007 Chicago Bears coach Lovie Smith becomes the first African American NFL coach to make it to the Super Bowl Championship.

2013 Barack Obama, the 44th President of the United States is sworn in for his second term as president.

 # JANUARY 22

1860 Politician, businessman, and free man of color, Walter Cohen is born in New Orleans, Louisiana. Cohen held appointments from three different presidents.

1866 Doctor and advocate for access to medical care for the Black community of Kansas City, Thomas Unthank is born in Greensboro, North Carolina.

1897 Blind gospel and blues musician and singer, Blind Willie Johnson is born in Independence, Texas.

JAN
FEB
MAR
APR
MAY
JUN
JUL
AUG
SEP
OCT
NOV
DEC

1922 The popular venue in Washington, D. C. for Black society, the Lincoln Theater opens its doors.

1931 Pioneering soul singer and songwriter Sam Cooke is born in Clarksdale, Mississippi. Cooke is remembered for his version of "You Send Me," "A Change is Gonna Come," and "Another Saturday Night."

2009 The Unites States Senate confirms Susan Rice as the first African American woman as Ambassador to the United Nations.

JANUARY 23

1837 African American evangelical preacher, missionary, and philanthropist, Amanda Smith is born a slave in Long Green, Maryland. In her later years Smith opens an orphanage for Black girls in Harvey, Illinois.

1889 African American doctor and surgeon Daniel H. Williams establishes Provident Hospital in Chicago, the first desegregated hospital in the U. S. Williams is also known for completing the first open heart surgery.

1964 The Twenty-fourth Amendment is passed, abolishing the poll tax as a condition for voting.

1977 The first episode of Alex Haley's *Roots* airs on national television.

1979 Nobel Peace Prize winner for

economics Afro Caribbean William A.

Lewis is born on the island of St. Lucia.

 ## JANUARY 24

1835 There is a Muslim slave revolt in Salvador da Bahia, Brazil, known as the Melê Revolt.

1874 The preeminent curator of Black history, Arthur Schomburg, is born in San Juan, Puerto Rico.

1908 African American humanitarian and diplomat John

Fredrick Thomas is born in Minneapolis, Minnesota. He was known especially for his work with refugees from WWII through the Vietnam War.

1962 The first African American Major League baseball player, Jackie Robinson is elected to the Baseball Hall of Fame.

JANUARY 25

1851 African American abolitionist and suffragist Sojourner Truth addresses the first Black Women's Rights Convention in Akron

Ohio with her "Ain't I a Woman?" speech.

1863 George Freeman Bragg, Jr., African American Episcopal priest, publisher and activist, is born in Warrenton, North Carolina.

1887 The forerunner of the NAACP, the Afro-American League is established by Timothy Thomas Fortune.

1911 African American pro football player, boxer, jazz bass player and drummer, Truck Parham is born in Chicago, Illinois.

1938 Powerhouse gospel, blues, and jazz singer, African American Etta James is born in Los Angeles, California.

1972 Shirley Chisholm announces her bid for the President of the United States. Chisholm becomes the first African American Presidential nominee and the first woman to run on the Democratic Party ticket.

Etta James memorialized at the Apollo Theatre's walk of fame

 # JANUARY 26

1863 54th Regiment of the U. S. Army is formed. It was known as the Black Infantry.

1892 The first woman pilot in the United States, African American Bessie Coleman is born in Atlanta, Texas.

1899 Playwright of social issues facing Blacks, May Miller is born in Washington, D. C.

1944 Outspoken African American activist Angela Davis is born in Birmingham, Alabama.

1948 President Harry Truman signs Executive Order 9981, which ends segregation in the US Military.

2020 Basketball great and philanthropist Kobe Bryant and his daughter Gianna are killed along with seven others when his helicopter crashes into a mountain in Calabasas, California.

 # JANUARY 27

1766 Hairstylist, businessman, humanitarian, and Haitian slave emigrant Pierre Toussaint is born in Saint-Domingue on Hispaniola.

1869 Violinist and composer of many popular songs of his day, African American Will Cook was born in Washington, D. C.

1894 The NFL's first African American coach, Fritz Pollard, is born in Chicago, Illinois.

1918 African American pioneering electric blues guitarist

JAN
FEB
MAR
APR
MAY
JUN
JUL
AUG
SEP
OCT
NOV
DEC

JAN
FEB
MAR
APR
MAY
JUN
JUL
AUG
SEP
OCT
NOV
DEC

Elmore James is born in Canton, Mississippi.

1939   Versatile African American

musician, author, and educator, Julius Lester is born in St. Louis Missouri.

 ## JANUARY 28

1778   White politician and abolitionist James Tallmadge, Jr. was born in Stanford, New York.

1862   African American medical missionary to Africa Louise Fleming is born in Hibernia Clay County, Florida.

1901   Elite sculptor Richmond Barthe is born in Bay Saint Louis, Mississippi.

1986   African American astronaut

Ronald E. McNair, along with the rest of the Space Shuttle Challenger crew, die in the explosion during launch.

2015   The convictions of 9 college students found guilty of trespassing and protesting by participating in a 1961 sit-in at a segregated lunch counter in Rock Hill, South Carolina were overturned.

  ## JANUARY 29

1820(22?)   Escaped slave and "Conductor"

on the Underground Railroad, Harriet

Tubman is born in Dorchester County, Maryland.

1872 African American Francis L. Cardoza is elected State Treasurer of South Carolina.

1907 A patent is granted to African American Henry Blair for his corn planter. Blair was unable to read or write, however he was thought to be a mechanical genius.

1940 African American poet, writer and educator Sterling Plumpp is born in Clinton, Mississippi.

1954 African American talk show host, entrepreneur, and billionaire Oprah Winfrey is born in Kosciusko, Mississippi.

1988 The Episcopal Church elects African American Barbara Harris the first woman bishop.

JANUARY 30

1832 The New England Anti-Slavery Society is established in Boston, Massachusetts.

1844 The first African American to graduate from Harvard, Richard T. Greener, is born in Philadelphia, Pennsylvania.

1858 The play "Escape," or "A Leap for Freedom" by William Wells Brown is published, one of the first plays published by an African American.

1944 The first African American woman to serve as mayor of Washington,

JAN
FEB
MAR
APR
MAY
JUN
JUL
AUG
SEP
OCT
NOV
DEC

JAN
FEB
MAR
APR
MAY
JUN
JUL
AUG
SEP
OCT
NOV
DEC

D. C., Sharon Pratt is born in Washington, D. C.

 ## JANUARY 31

1914 African American World heavyweight boxing campion Jersey Joe Walcott (given name Arnold Cream) is born in Merchantville, New Jersey.

1919 Seminal baseball great and first African American to integrate major league baseball Jackie Robinson is born in Cairo, Georgia.

1921 Broadway star, singer and actress Carol Channing is born in Seattle, Washington. Her father was a light-skinned Black.

1931 Record-breaking and Baseball Hall of Famer, African American Ernie Banks is born in Dallas, Texas.

1934 Singer Etta Moten is the first African American to perform at the White House in the 20th century.

1988 Washington Redskins' Doug Williams is the first African American NFL quarterback to receive the Superbowl Most Valuable Player award.

FEBRUARY 1

1810 African American abolitionist and lecturer Charles Remond is born in Salem, Massachusetts.

1865 The first African American to be admitted to the bar of the Supreme Court of the United States, John Rock, is born in Salem, New Jersey.

1867 The first African American to hold public office in South Carolina, Francis Cardozo is born in Charleston, South Carolina.

1894 Innovative African American pianist and composer James P. Johnson is born in New Brunswick, New Jersey.

1960 The sit-in at Woolworths in Greensboro, North Carolina by four African American college students sparks a movement throughout the southeast, bringing to light the segregation laws and policies of the south.

1902 Esteemed African American poet, author, and social commentator Langston Hughes is born in Joplin, Missouri.

 # FEBRUARY 2

1827 African American abolitionist, businessman and inventor John P. Parker

JAN
FEB
MAR
APR
MAY
JUN
JUL
AUG
SEP
OCT
NOV
DEC

is born in Norfolk, Virginia.

1897 The patent for the ice cream scoop is given to African American inventor Alfred Cralle.

1914 Black sculptor and pottery artist William Ellsworth Artis is born in Washington, North Carolina.

1915 Ernest Just receives the NAACP Spingarn Medal for his research on cell division.

1924 Accomplished African American jazz saxophonist Sonny Stitt is born in Boston, Massachusetts.

2009 Eric Holder becomes the first African American Untied States Attorney General.

 # FEBRUARY 3

1811 Staunch white abolitionist and editor Horace Greeley is born in Amherst, New Hampshire.

1867 African American zoologist and teacher Charles Turner is born in Cincinnati, Ohio.

1870 15th Amendment to the Constitution, the Voting Rights Act, is ratified by Congress, giving Black men the right to vote.

1957 Award-winning documentary filmmaker African American Marlon Riggs is born in Fort Worth, Texas.

1965 African American sculptor Geraldine McCullough wins Widener Gold Medal.

 # FEBRUARY 4

1794 France abolishes slavery.

1931 Honored civil rights activist Rosa Parks is born in Tuskegee, Alabama. Parks refused to give up her seat on the bus to a white man, exposing discrimination and racism in the United States.

1948 African American security guard of the Watergate Hotel Frank Wills is born in Savannah, Georgia. Wills caught burglars wiretapping the phones of the Democratic National Committee, eventually causing the downfall of President Richard Nixon.

1989 Nkosi Johnson is born with HIV/AIDS in South Africa. With the help of his foster mother, Nkosi becomes an outspoken advocate for HIV/AIDS health care in South Africa. He died in 2001.

1999 Four New York plainclothes policeman shoot an unarmed student from Guinea, Amadou Diallo, killing him instantly.

2006 Warren Moon becomes the first African American NFL quarterback to be entered into the NFL Hall of Fame.

JAN
FEB
MAR
APR
MAY
JUN
JUL
AUG
SEP
OCT
NOV
DEC

JAN
FEB
MAR
APR
MAY
JUN
JUL
AUG
SEP
OCT
NOV
DEC

FEBRUARY 5

1813 Underground Railroad conductor and minister African American Jermain Wesley Loguen is born in Davidson County, Tennessee.

1836 Politician and the first African American congressman to speak in Georgia's House of Representatives, Jefferson Long is born in Knoxville, Tennessee.

1858 Advocate of education for Blacks and minister African American Henry Delany is born in Saint Mary's, Georgia.

1934 One of the greatest men to ever play baseball, African American Hank Aaron was born in Mobile, Alabama.

1994 After 31 years Klansman Byron De La Beckwith is found guilty of the assassination of Black civil rights activist Medgar Evers and sentenced to life in prison.

A statue of Hank Aaron hitting a baseball at Truist Park in Atlanta, Georgia

FEBRUARY 6

1882 African American poet Anne Spence is born in Henry County, Virginia.

1820 The first organized group of freed slaves emigrate from New York to Sierra Leone.

1867 The Peabody Education Fund is established by white philanthropist George Peabody for the education of Blacks in the South.

1905 The first African American woman to attend Oxford University, Merze Tate, is born in Blanchard, Michigan.

1945 Legendary reggae and ska musician and social activist Bob Marley is born in the Parish of St. Ann, Jamaica.

1993 The first number 1 ranked Black tennis player in the world and HIV/AIDS advocate Arthur Ashe dies from complications due to AIDS. It is believed that he contracted AIDS from a blood transfusion.

 # FEBRUARY 7

1862 Freedman's Aid Society is formed to provide education and support for freed slaves.

JAN
FEB
MAR
APR
MAY
JUN
JUL
AUG
SEP
OCT
NOV
DEC

1887 Ragtime pianist and composer Eubie Blake is born in Baltimore, Maryland.

1926 Instituted by Carter Woodson, the first National Negro Week is celebrated, which in 1976 develops into Black History Month.

1933 Promising professional football player Cal Jones is born in Steubenville, Ohio. He died at 23 years old in a plane crash in Canada.

1943 Brilliant physicist, author, and educator Ronald Mickens is born in Petersburg, Virginia.

1966 Award-winning comedian and entertainer Chris Rock is born in Georgetown, South Carolina.

 # FEBRUARY 8

1831 The first African American Woman to receive a medical degree in the U. S., Rebecca Crumpler is born in Delaware.

1924 Ada Sipuel (Fisher) is born in Chickasha, Oklahoma. Sipuel sued for inclusion at the University of Oklahoma Law School, eventually becoming the first African American woman to attend a southern all-white law school.

1924 Powerhouse pitcher in the Negro Leagues and for the Brooklyn Dodgers Joe Black is born in Plainfield, New Jersey.

JAN
FEB
MAR
APR
MAY
JUN
JUL
AUG
SEP
OCT
NOV
DEC

1931 African American advocate for equal housing and other social issues Katie McWatt is born in Minneapolis, Minnesota.

1968 Three students, Samuel Hammond, Jr., Delano Middleton, and Henry Smith are killed, and 27 others were injured in the Orangeburg Massacre at South Carolina State University.

 # FEBRUARY 9

1902 African American singer and bandleader Blanche Calloway is born in Baltimore, Maryland. Her brother, Cab Calloway, was also a prominent singer and bandleader.

1943 African American singer and song writer Barbara Lewis is born in South Lyon, Michigan. Lewis is best known for her song "Hello Stranger."

1944 Author of *The Color Purple*, and other novels of historical fiction, African American Alice Walker is born in Eatonton, Georgia.

1971 Monumental African American pro baseball player Satchel Paige is inducted into the Baseball Hall of Fame.

1995 Bernard Harris, Jr. becomes the first African American astronaut to walk in space.

FEBRUARY 10

1874 African American Lewis Latimer, and Charles W. Brown receive a patent for water closets on passenger cars on trains.

1903 White Jewish-American poet and writer of the powerful poem turned into song "Strange Fruit," and others Abel Meeropol is born in the Bronx, New York.

1907 The first African American woman to serve in Georgia House of Representatives, Grace Hamilton is born in Atlanta, Georgia.

1909 One of the most famous drummers of all time, African American William Henry "Chick" Webb is born in Baltimore, Maryland.

1927 Legendary African American soprano Leontyne Price is born in Laurel, Mississippi.

1964 The Civil Rights Act of 1964, making it illegal to discriminate based on color, race, sex, religion, or national origin, is passed in the United States House of Representatives.

 # FEBRUARY 11

1871 Accomplished African American librarian and writer

Edward C. Williams is born in Cleveland, Ohio.

1897 The White Rose Home for Colored Working Girls is founded in New York City. Also known as the White Rose Mission, it operated for over 80 years.

1915 Influential African American blues and folk singer Josh White is born in Greenville, South Carolina.

1920 One of the original Tuskegee Airmen and the first African American four-star General in the U. S. Military, Daniel James is born in Pensacola, Florida.

1977 The first Black Secretary of State, Clifford Alexander, is confirmed.

1990 After 27 years in a South African prison, Nelson Mandela is released.

📑 FEBRUARY 12

1793 The first Fugitive Slave Law is passed by Congress. This law allowed slave owners to recapture their fugitive slaves in free states.

1809 Abraham Lincoln, sixteenth president of the United States and executor of the Emancipation Proclamation, is born.

1900 "Lift Every Voice and Sing," by James and Rosamond Johnson, is performed at the Colored High School in Jacksonville, Florida to celebrate Abraham Lincoln's birthday. It becomes

JAN
FEB
MAR
APR
MAY
JUN
JUL
AUG
SEP
OCT
NOV
DEC

the "Negro National Anthem."

1907   African American gospel singer and composer Roberta Martin is born in Helena, Arkansas.

1909   The National Association for the Advancement of Colored People (NAACP) is organized to help further the cause of civil rights in the United States.

1934   African American basketball great and Olympic gold medalist in basketball, Bill Russell is born in Monroe, Louisiana.

 # FEBRUARY 13

1873   Journalist and personal secretary to Booker T. Washington, African American Emmett J. Scott is born in Houston, Texas.

1908   The first Black network news reporter on TV, Malvin Goode is born in White Plains, Virginia.

1920   The National Negro League is formed in Kansas City to create an African American baseball league.

1923   The first all-Black basketball team, the Renaissance, is organized in Harlem, New York.

1960   Sit-ins at lunch counters begin in Nashville, Tennessee to protest segregation and inequality in the south.

1967 The New York Stock Exchange admits Clarence B. Jones as its first African American member.

....

 # FEBRUARY 14

1760 First bishop of the AME Church, Richard Allen is born in Philadelphia, Pennsylvania.

....

1817 Although his actual birthdate is unknown, celebrated African American abolitionist and social activist Fredrick Douglass celebrated his birth on February 14.

....

1880 African American vaudeville star, singer, dancer, and choreographer, Aida Walker, is born in New York City.

....

1894 Founder of the National Negro Opera Company, Mary Dawson is born in Meridian, North Carolina.

....

1946 African American actor, singer, dancer, and entertainer, Gregory Hines is born in New York, New York.

....

1957 The Southern Christian Leadership Conference is organized with Martin Luther King, Jr. as president.

....

FEBRUARY 15

1820 Leading national suffragist and active white abolitionist, Susan B. Anthony is born in Adams, Massachusetts.

1851 Shadrach Minkins is rescued by Black abolitionists while he was being held in accordance with the 1850 Fugitive Slave Law.

1865 Lawyer and politician, George Lawrence Mabson enlists in the Union Army. Mabson served in the North Carolina House of Representatives and was North Carolina's first Black attorney.

1913 Gospel music composer African American Louise Jarrett Shropshire is born in Coffee County, Alabama.

1942 Creator of ad campaigns for Good Year, Campbells Soup, Kentucky Fried Chicken (KFC), and others, African American Caroline Jones is born in Benton Harbor Michigan.

1944 Director of the National Health Law Program and the Office of Civil Rights, African American Sylvia Drew Ivie is born in Washington, D. C.

2011 Maya Angelou, prolific African American author, educator, and civil rights activist Maya Angelou receives the Presidential Medal of Freedom from President Barack Obama.

Maya Angelou delivers a poem on Bill Clinton's Inauguration Day, January 20, 1993, in Washington, DC

JAN
FEB
MAR
APR
MAY
JUN
JUL
AUG
SEP
OCT
NOV
DEC

FEBRUARY 16

1904 The first live actor to be hired by Walt Disney, James Baskett is born in Indianapolis, Indiana. African American Baskett received an honorary Oscar for his portrayal of Uncle Remus in Walt Disney's *Song of the South*.

1931 African American Otis Blackwell, premiere song writer for Elvis Presley, Jerry Lee Lewis, The Who, and Otis Redding, among others, is born. Blackwell's most famous songs include "All Shook Up," "Great Balls of Fire," and "Return to Sender."

1957 Actor and TV host LeVar Burton is born in Landstuhl, Germany. Burton is best known for his roles as Kunta Kinte in the miniseries *Roots*, the host of *Reading Rainbow* and Geordi LaForge in *Star Trek: The Next Generation*.

1961 Chicago opens a museum in honor of

Jean Baptiste DuSable, the African Haitian who settled the outpost at the edge of Lake Michigan, eventually becoming the city of Chicago.

1970 In the "Fight of the Century," Joe Frazier beat Muhammad Ali, to become the World Heavyweight Boxing Champion.

 # FEBRUARY 17

1874 Historian of African American and folk music and teacher Maud Hare is born in Galveston, Texas.

1916 African American Union activist and Congressman Charles Hayes is born in Cairo, Illinois.

1936 Football player, actor, and founder of the Amer-I-Can organization, African American Jim Brown is born in Saint Simons, Georgia.

1938 African American lawyer, activist and member of the Civil Rights Commission, Mary Frances Berry is born in Nashville, Tennessee.

1963 Phenomenal basketball player, team owner, and Presidential Medal of Freedom recipient, African American Michael Jordan is born in Brooklyn, New York.

1973 The Naval ship USS Jesse L. Brown is commissioned. The ship is named in honor of Ensign Jesse Brown, the

first African American
Naval pilot to die in
the Korean War.

1942 Founder of the
Black Panther Party,
Huey Newton is born in
Louisiana.

 # FEBRUARY 18

1688 First
antislavery resolution
passed in Germantown,
Pennsylvania by the
Quakers.

1867 The Augusta
Institute is established
in Augusta, Georgia.
The college moved to
Atlanta in 1897 and
is currently known as
the prestigious HBCU
Morehouse College.

1894 "Architect to
the Stars" African
American Paul Revere
Williams is born in Los
Angeles, California.

1931 Award-winning
writer Toni Morrison
is born in Lorain,
Ohio. Morrison's works

centered on the African
American experience.

1950 Award-winning
and best-selling
African American
author Bebe More is
born in Philadelphia,
Pennsylvania.

2006 Shani Davis
wins a Winter Olympic
gold medal in the
men's 1000-meter
speedskating event.
He is the first African
American athlete to win
a winter gold medal in
an individual sport.

JAN
FEB
MAR
APR
MAY
JUN
JUL
AUG
SEP
OCT
NOV
DEC

FEBRUARY 19

1869 Assistant to Booker T. Washington for the Pan-African conference, Sylvester Williams is born in Trinidad.

1871 African American social organizer and civil rights activist Lugenia B. Hope is born in St. Louis, Missouri.

1902 African American vaudeville tap dancer, originator of "jazz tap," John Sublett "Bubbles" is born in Louisville, Kentucky.

1918 W.E.B. DuBois heads the First Pan-African Congress in Paris, France.

1983 The highest ranking Black female graduate of West Point and recipient of the Purple Heart, Bronze Star Medal, and others, Emily Perez is born. Perez is killed in combat on September 12, 2006, in Kifl, Iraq.

2002 Bobsledder Vonetta Flowers becomes the first African American to receive an Olympic gold medal in the Winter Olympics.

 # FEBRUARY 20

1895 Influential African American abolitionist and civil rights advocate Fredrick Douglass dies in Washington, D.C.

1898 African American James Yancey, influential Boogie-Woogie pianist and composer, is born in Chicago, Illinois.

1927 Oscar winning Black actor and Bahamian ambassador Sidney Poitier is born in Miami, Florida.

1962 Writer for DC, Marvel, and Archie comics African American Dwayne McDuffie is born in Detroit, Michigan.

1988 African American popstar and fashion icon Rihanna is born in ST. Michael Parish, Barbados.

 # FEBRUARY 21

1862 The only person to be convicted as a slave trader in the United States, Nathaniel Gordon is executed by hanging.

1909 Philadelphia's first African American licensed doctor of obstetrics and gynecology, Helen Octavia Dickens, is born in Dayton, Ohio

1917 African American jazz pianist, composer, and bandleader Tadd Dameron is born in Cleveland, Ohio.

1933 Dynamic soul singer, African American Nina Simone, born Eunice Kathleen Waymon, is born in Tryon, North Carolina.

1936 The first African American congresswoman from the south, Barbara Jordan is born in Houston, Texas.

JAN
FEB
MAR
APR
MAY
JUN
JUL
AUG
SEP
OCT
NOV
DEC

JAN
FEB
MAR
APR
MAY
JUN
JUL
AUG
SEP
OCT
NOV
DEC

REPUBLIQUE DE GUINEE
Office de la Poste Guinéenne 2010
5000 FG.
2010
Nina Simone
Chanteuses américaines

Nina Simone on a postage stamp of Guinea

1961 African American Otis Boykin receives a patent for his electronic resistor. Boykin later receives a patent for a pacemaker controller.

1965 African American human rights activist and civil rights leader Malcom X is assassinated.

 # FEBRUARY 22

1841 Known best for his depictions of the American West, artist and lithographer African American Grafton Tyler Brown is born in Harrisburg, Pennsylvania.

1881 African American bandleader, composer, and musical innovator, James R. Europe is born in Mobile, Alabama.

1888 Notable African American folk artist Horace Pippin is born in West Chester, Pennsylvania.

1935 The iconic nightclub, the Village

Vanguard Jazz Club opens in Greenwich Village, New York.

....

1950 Basketball superstar Julius Erving is born in East Meadow, New York.

....

1989 The first rap Grammy award is given to DJ Jazzy Jeff and the Fresh Prince (Will Smith) for "Parents Just Don't Understand."

....

 # FEBRUARY 23

1868 Influential author, educator and historian W. E. B. DuBois is born.

....

1925 Fifteen-time elected congressman African American Louis Stokes is born in Cleveland, Ohio.

....

1929 New York Yankees outfielder and the first African American to win the American League MVP award, Elston Howard is born in St. Louis, Missouri.

....

1937 Best-selling author of *Manchild in the Promised Land* African American Claude Brown is born in New York City.

....

1979 Frank E. Peterson becomes the first African American U. S. Marine Corps brigadier general.

....

1983 African American Harold Washington wins the Democratic party nomination for Chicago mayor.

....

JAN
FEB
MAR
APR
MAY
JUN
JUL
AUG
SEP
OCT
NOV
DEC

Virginia Holocaust Museum in the shockoe slip area of Richmond, Virginia

 # FEBRUARY 24

1811 Reformer, educator and Bishop of the AME Church, Daniel Payne is born in Charleston, South Carolina.

1864 Rebecca Crumpler is the first African American Woman to receive a medical degree in the U. S.

1873 Expert stone mason and bricklayer African American Casiville Bullard is born in Memphis, Tennessee.

1931 African American civil rights activist Lillie Brown is born in Troy, Alabama.

1944 Known as the "Golden Thirteen," 13 African American seamen become the first U. S. Naval officers.

1983 Shockoe Bottom, a former major slave trading center in Richmond, VA, is declared an historical site by the National Trust for Historic Preservation.

FEBRUARY 25

1826 Lawyer and desegregationist African American Alexander G. Clark is born. In 1867 Clark sued the Muscatine School District to allow his daughter to attend and won.

1837 Cheyney State University, the first institution of higher learning for Blacks and HBCU, is founded through the bequest of Richard Humphreys.

1870 Hiram Revels is sworn in as the first Black man to be seated in the US Senate.

1896 The Albany Bible and Manual Training Institute, known today as Albany State University, an HBUC is established.

1914 Black Holocaust Museum founder James Cameron is born in La Crosse, Wisconsin. The museum chronicles lynchings in the United States.

1928 African American Federal judge Aloysius Higginbotham is born in Trenton, New Jersey. Higginbotham received the Presidential Medal of Freedom in 1995 from Pres. Bill Clinton.

 # FEBRUARY 26

JAN
FEB
MAR
APR
MAY
JUN
JUL
AUG
SEP
OCT
NOV
DEC

JAN
FEB
MAR
APR
MAY
JUN
JUL
AUG
SEP
OCT
NOV
DEC

1844 African American two-time Congressman James E. O'Hara is born in New York City.

1872 Cookman Institute, now HBCU Bethune-Cookman University, is established in Jacksonville, Florida.

1943 African American actor and director Bill Duke is born in Poughkeepsie, New York.

2007 The American Press Corps honors Frederick Douglass for his historic contributions to the field of journalism.

 # FEBRUARY 27

1853 The first Black YMCA chapter is established.

1869 John Willis Menard is the first African American to address the U. S. House of Representatives.

1872 Charlotte Ray graduates from Howard University to become the first Black woman lawyer.

1897 Ground-breaking African American singer, Marian Anderson is born in Philadelphia, Pennsylvania. Records indicate this is her correct birthdate, however Anderson insisted that the actual date was February 17, 1902.

1988 Debi Thomas wins the first Winter Olympics medal by an African American by winning a bronze medal for figure skating.

 FEBRUARY 28

1704 Frenchman Elias Neau establishes the first school for Blacks in New York.

1895 Bluefield Colored Institute, now known as Bluefield State University, an HBCU, is established in Bluefield, West Virginia.

1966 Andrew Brimmer is nominated as the first African American member of the Board of Governors for the Federal Reserve by President Lyndon Johnson.

1968 Marine Corps Private, First-Class James Anderson, Jr., gave his life in sacrifice for the life of others in the military conflict of Vietnam. He was the first African American Marine to receive the Congressional Medal of Honor for his heroism.

2003 Ku Klux Klan member Ernest Avants is convicted of the 1966 murder of Ben White. Avants is sentenced to life in prison.

 FEBRUARY 29

JAN
FEB
MAR
APR
MAY
JUN
JUL
AUG
SEP
OCT
NOV
DEC

1892 African American artist and sculptor Augusta Savage is born in Green Cove Springs, Florida

1948 African American fashion designer Willi Smith is born in Philadelphia, Pennsylvania.

1968 The Kerner Commission Report finds that in southern school districts only 22% of Black students are in integrated schools.

2004 After international pressure and riots in Haiti, President Jean-Bertrand Aristide resigns and seeks refuge for exile.

The Brown v. Board of Education National Historic Site in Topeka, Kansas

MARCH 1

1780 Pennsylvania becomes the second state to abolish slavery.

1875 The Civil Rights Bill was passed, declared "all men equal before the law" which made it illegal to discriminate in places of public accommodation (restaurants, hotels, etc.).

1890 The California Supreme Court rules that Visalia School District must allow for segregated schools in Wysinger v. Crookshank. This ruling was used to support the case of Brown v. Board of Education.

1896 The first Italo-Ethiopian War ends with the Treaty of Addis Ababa, when Ethiopia's army of 100,000 troops overwhelmed the roughly 14,500 Italian troops.

1927 Award-winning Jamaican American singer, entertainer and civil rights activist Harry Belafonte is born in New York.

 # MARCH 2

1867 Howard University, one of the Historically Black Colleges and Universities, is founded in Washington, D.C.

1888 The first Black-controlled bank, the

Savings Bank of the Grand Fountain United Order of the True Reformers, is founded.

1919 The Associated Negro Press is started by Claude Barnett in Chicago, Illinois.

1955 African American Claudette Colvin is arrested for refusing to give up her seat on a Montgomery, Alabama bus. Fifteen-year-old Claudette is tried and convicted for her offense, nine months before Rosa Parks is arrested.

1962 One of the greatest basketball players of all time, African American Wilt Chamberlain, scores a record breaking 100 points in a single NBA game.

 # MARCH 3

1819 Episcopalian missionary and first African American to graduate from Queens College, Cambridge, England Alexander Crummell is born.

1820 The Missouri Compromise is ratified by Congress. The "compromise" was to keep free and slave territories balanced in the acquisition of new states.

1859 to settle the debts of Pierce Butler the largest sale of slaves in U. S. history, known as "the weeping time," occurs in Savannah, Georgia.

1865 An act of Congress founds The Freedmen's

Bureau to help with the displacement of formerly enslaved people after the Civil War.

1891 The Elizabeth City State Colored Normal School, later called Elizabeth City State University, an

HBUC, is established for the training of African American teachers.

1991 Rodney King is caught on video being beaten by 4 police officers after a traffic stop in Los Angeles, California.

 MARCH 4

1834 African American Nancy Hayes Green, also known as Aunt Jemima, is born. As Aunt Jemima, Green became a living trademark for the brand.

1867 The first licensed African American woman dentist, Ida Gray Nelson Rollins, is born in Clarksville, Tennessee.

1877 African American inventor of the traffic signal and gas mask, Garrett Morgan is born in Paris Kentucky.

1890 The town of Langston, Oklahoma is founded by Edwin and Sarah McCabe as a Black settlement.

1903 Publisher of the Clarion newspaper in Nova Scotia, Carrie Best is born. The

Clarion is Nova Scotia's first Black newspaper.

1916 Athlete and champion for racial equality African American Homer Harris is born in Seattle, Washington.

 MARCH 5

1770 An escaped slave, Crispus Attucks, is the first victim of the Boston Massacre.

1897 The American Negro Academy is established in Washington, D. C. to promote education within the Black community.

1939 Highly-acclaimed African American playwright Charles Fuller is born in Philadelphia, Pennsylvania.

1947 Political and civil rights activist African American Bernard Powell is born in Kansas City.

 MARCH 6

1797 Resolute white abolitionist Gerrit Smith is born in Utica, New York. Smith used much of his wealth providing for those in the Black community and supporting the cause of emancipation.

1857 The Supreme Court denies blacks US citizenship in the Dred Scott decision.

The ruling also denied Congress to restrict slavery in federal territories.

. . . .

1882 The Virginia Normal and Collegiate Institute is established. It is now known as Virginia State University, HBCU.

. . . .

1942 The first five of the Tuskegee Airmen graduate from the Tuskegee Flight school, African Americans;

Lemuel R. Custis, Charles DeBow, Mac Ross, George Spencer Roberts, and Benjamin O. Davis.

. . . .

1957 Ghana, formerly the Gold Coast, secures independence from Great Britain.

. . . .

1972 Accomplished African American basketball star Shaquille O'Neal is born in Newark, New Jersey.

. . . .

 ## MARCH 7

Basketball stars Ron Artest and Shaq O'Neal

JAN
FEB
MAR
APR
MAY
JUN
JUL
AUG
SEP
OCT
NOV
DEC

JAN
FEB

MAR
APR
MAY
JUN
JUL
AUG
SEP
OCT
NOV

DEC

1897 Author and abolitionist Harriet Jacobs is born a slave. She is educated as a child, escapes slavery and publishes her experiences in the book *Incidents in Life of a Slave Girl.*

1917 The first African American to dance at the Metropolitan Opera House, Janet Collins, is born. Collins was a prima ballerina and artist.

1942 Anarchist and labor reformer African American Lucy Parsons dies in a house fire.

1965 Civil rights advocates marching from Selma to Montgomery, Alabama are met with physical violence from the Alabama State Police, hospitalizing over 50 protesters.

1979 The state of Georgia apologizes 18 years after Ray Charles refuses to perform for a segregated audience in Augusta, Georgia. At the time he was sued and fined for breach of contract.

 # MARCH 8

1825 Alexander Thomas Augusta, the first African American doctor in the U. S. Army is born. Augusta becomes the highest- ranking Army officer up to that time.

1866 African American Thomas Fountain Blue, the librarian who establishes the first library for Blacks, is born.

....

1900 Notable African American poet and teacher Marcus B. Christian is born.

....

1902 Prolific African American movie and TV actress Louise Beavers is born.

....

1911 African American Clarence Mitchell, Jr. civil rights lobbyist for the NAACP from 1950-1978, is born in Baltimore, Maryland.

....

1964 Malcom X splits from the Nation of Islam.

....

MARCH 9

1841 The Supreme Court grants those aboard the slave ship Amistad their freedom.

....

1871 The first African American congressman from the North, Oscar Stanton De Priest is born in Florence, Alabama.

....

1891 The Agricultural and Mechanical College for the Colored Race, now North Carolina Agricultural and Technical State University, is founded. North Carolina A&T is an HBCU.

....

1922 African American civil rights activist, lawyer, and developer Floyd McKissick is born in Ashville, North Carolina.

....

1930 Respected jazz musician and composer African American

JAN FEB MAR APR MAY JUN JUL AUG SEP OCT NOV DEC

Ornette Coleman is born in Fort Worth, Texas.

 ## MARCH 10

1779 The hymn "Amazing Grace" written by slave trader turned British abolitionist John Newton is published.

1850 Author, educator, and activist Hallie Quinn is born in Pittsburgh, Pennsylvania.

1784 Co-founder of the National Bar Association, African American Charles P. Howard, Sr. is born in Abbeville, South Carolina.

1913 The indomitable Harriet Tubman, leader in the Underground Railroad, dies in Auburn, New York.

1972 Over 8,000 African Americans gather for the first National Black Political Assembly held in Gary Indiana.

 ## MARCH 11

1878 Prairie View A&M School for Colored Youth, now known as Prairie View A&M University, welcomes its first 8 students.

1926 Southern Baptist minister and associate of Martin

Luther King, Jr. Ralph Abernathy, Sr. is born.

....

1943 Brazilian politician and activist Benedita da Silva is born. Born in the slums of Rio de Janeiro, she becomes the first Afro Brazilian woman governor in Brazil.

....

1950 Singular African American vocal performer Bobby McFerrin is born. McFerrin is best known for his song "Don't Worry, Be Happy."

....

1959 Larraine Hansberry's award-winning play "A Raisin in the Sun" debuts on Broadway. It is the first Broadway produced play written by an African American woman.

....

Bobby McFerrin performs at the festival JazzFestBrno on March 30, 2011, in Brno, Czech republic

 # MARCH 12

1897 The Colored Agricultural and Normal College, currently Langston University, is established in Langston, Oklahoma.

....

1926 The iconic Savoy Ballroom opens in Harlem, New York.

1932 African American Civil rights leader, politician, and aide to Martin Luther King, Jr., Andrew Jackson Young is born in New Orleans, Louisiana.

1934 Award-winning children's author Virginia Hamilton is born. Hamilton is the first African American author to receive the prestigious Newbery Medal for children's literature.

 # MARCH 13

1774 The first woman police officer in North America, African Nova Scotian Rose Fortune, is born.

1872 White civil rights advocate and NAACP supporter Oswald Villard is born.

1881 African American ragtime pianist Louis Chauvin is born.

1962 Prolific composer and jazz trumpeter African American Terence Blanchard is born.

1972 African American Lonnie Corant Lynn, professionally known as Common, a rapper and actor, is born.

MARCH 14

1793 African American inventor Eli Whitney is granted a patent for the cotton gin.

1914 Brazilian Black civil rights activist and politician Abdias so Nascimento is born.

1923 African Chief and national hero of Namibia, Samuel Maharero, is born.

1960 African American Baseball Hall of Famer Kirby Puckett is born.

 # MARCH 15

1809 The first president of the African country of Liberia, Joseph Jenkins Roberts, is born in Norfolk, Virginia. Roberts emigrated to Liberia in 1829.

1858 Soldier, barber, prominent citizen and one of the first Black police officers in Kansas City, Lafayette A. Tillman is born in Evansville, Indiana.

1910 Actor and co-founder of the Ebony Showcase Theater, Nick Stewart, is born in New York City.

1946 Standout professional baseball player Bobby Bonds is born. Bobby Bonds is the father of baseball great Barry Bonds.

JAN
FEB
MAR
APR
MAY
JUN
JUL
AUG
SEP
OCT
NOV
DEC

1999 Maurice Ashley becomes the first Black chess player to achieve International Grand Master status.

Maurice Ashley & Eric Gonzales at an afterschool chess program for Bed-Stuy elementary students

MARCH 16

1827 The first newspaper produced by Blacks, *Freedom's Journal*, is published.

1846 The first African American to graduate from the Women's Medical College of Pennsylvania, and the second African American woman to receive her medical doctorate in the U.S., Rebecca Cole, is born.

1870 The first African American legislator to sit in either the Senate or Congress, Senator Hiram Rhodes Revels, makes his first speech in the senate.

1906 Joseph Bass publishes the first edition of

his newspaper for Blacks, *The Montana Plaindealer.*

1991 Latasha Harlins is shot and dies in a Koreatown, Los Angeles liquor store. The owner of the store was convicted of manslaughter and sentenced to 5 years of probation.

MARCH 17

1806 The African American inventor of modern sugar refining techniques, Norbert Rillieux, is born.

1825 The first African American to elected to the House of Representatives from Alabama, Benjamin Turner is born.

1863 African American civil rights activist, Homer Plessy, is born. Plessy brought the case of Plessy v. Ferguson to the Supreme Court, which ruled separate but equal does not infringe on the 14th Amendment.

1885 Ada Crogman Franklin, performing arts administer, and editor, is born in Atlanta, GA. Franklin is famous for her national production of the history and contributions of Blacks in the United States in the play, *Milestones of a Race.*

1912 Civil rights leader Bayard Rustin is born. Rustin was an aide to Martin Luther King, Jr., and a key player in the organization of the March on Washington.

1919 Preeminent popular jazz vocalist, pianist, and father to singer Natlie Cole, Nathaniel Adams Cole, Nat King Cole, is born in Montgomery, Alabama.

 # MARCH 18

1922 Ordained African American minister and civil rights leader Fred Shuttlesworth is born. Shuttlesworth is one of the founders of the Alabama Christian Movement for Human Rights, when the NAACP was outlawed in that state.

1933 Unita Zelma Blackwell, the first African American woman mayor in Mississippi, is born in Lula, Mississippi.

1938 Award-winning African American poet Michael S. Harper

is born in Brooklyn, New York. His poems focus on the African American experience.

1941 Rock and Roll Hall of Famer African American Wilson Pickett is born in Prattville, Alabama

1970 African American hip-hop artist and singer turned actor Queen Latifah, born Dana Elaine Owens, is born in Newark, New Jersey.

MARCH 19

1813 British explorer and abolitionist David Livingstone is born. Although a staunch believer in emancipation, he had many misguided dealings in Africa that supported the slave trade.

1891 The first African American teacher and principal appointed in Los Angeles Public Schools Bessie Burke is born.

1935 The Harlem race riot of 1935 is one of the first and largest post-Civil War race riots in the nation. More than 10,000 people protest on the mistaken assumption that a Black Puerto Rican teen was beaten and killed for stealing a pen knife.

1966 Texas Western University Miners become the first NCAA basketball team to start with 5 Black players against a team with 5 white players in the championship. The Miners won the NCAA tournament.

 # MARCH 20

1883 African American Jan Matzeliger is granted a patent for a machine that makes a complete shoe.

JAN
FEB
MAR
APR
MAY
JUN
JUL
AUG
SEP
OCT
NOV
DEC

1920 African American religious and community artist Allen Crite is born in North Plainfield, New Jersey.

1934 California politician and the first African American mayor of San Francisco, Willie Brown is born in Mineola, Texas.

1957 Oscar-winning African American actor, director, and producer of films with social commentary Spike (Sheldon Jackson) Lee is born in Atlanta, Georgia.

Spike Lee at the photocall for *Blackkklansman* at the 71st Festival de Cannes

 # MARCH 21

1960 The Sharpsville Massacre in South Africa ends with police killing more than 70 Blacks and wounding an estimated 150 others.

1965 Martin Luther King, Jr. leads a group of 2,000 marchers in the Selma Freedom March from Selma, Alabama to Montgomery.

1990 Namibia, previously South Africa, achieves independence from Germany.

 ## MARCH 22

1856 The first African American graduate of West Point Henry Flipper is born in Thomasville, Georgia.

1873 Slavery is abolished in Puerto Rico.

1893 African American artist and printing innovator Dox Thrash is born in Griffin, Georgia.

1906 The most reliable worker recorded by the U. S. Department of Labor, Arthur Winston, is born. He retired on his 100th birthday, missing only one day for his wife's funeral, in his 72-year work history.

2002 Amina Kurami is sentenced to stoning to death for adultery in an Islamic court in Nigeria. After global protest and a retrial with legal representation, Kurami is acquitted of the charges.

 ## MARCH 23

1906 African American teacher and civil rights advocate Aline Black is born in Norfolk, Virginia.

JAN
FEB
MAR
APR
MAY
JUN
JUL
AUG
SEP
OCT
NOV
DEC

1938 The first African American mayor of Atlanta, Georgia Maynard Jackson is born in Dallas, Texas.

1991 The eleven-year civil war in Sierra Leon begins.

 ## MARCH 24

1912 Civil rights and social activist African American Dorothy Irene Height is born.

1914 Noted African American sportswriter and ardent supporter of sports integration Wendell Smith is born in Detroit, Michigan.

1971 The Southern Regional Council declares school desegregation in the south is beginning to take hold.

2002 Halle Berry wins the first Oscar for best actress awarded to an African American woman for her role as Leticia Musgrove in *Monster's Ball*.

1966 In the case Harper v. Virginia the Supreme Court ruled poll taxes are unconstitutional. Poll taxes were established in some southern states to discourage Blacks from voting.

MARCH 25

1900 African American psychologist and social worker Ruth W. Howard is born in Washington, D. C.

1931 Nine Black teenage boys, known as the Scottsboro Boys, are wrongly accused, and arrested for attacking two white girls.

1942 Incomparable soul and jazz singer Aretha Franklin is born in Detroit, Michigan. Franklin is best known for her rendition of the Otis Redding song "Respect."

1949 The first African American woman U. S. Naval Rear Admiral Lillian Fishburne is born in Patuxent River, Maryland.

1967 African American Olympic figure skater and surgeon Debi Thomas is born in Poughkeepsie, New York.

 # MARCH 26

1870 William T. Francis is born in Indianapolis, Indiana

1872 A patent is given to African American Thomas J. Martin for his improvements to the fire extinguisher.

JAN
FEB
MAR
APR
MAY
JUN
JUL
AUG
SEP
OCT
NOV
DEC

JAN
FEB

MAR

APR
MAY
JUN
JUL
AUG
SEP
OCT
NOV
DEC

1882 Postal clerk and civil rights advocate John Wesley Dobbs is born in Marietta, Georgia.

1937 President Franklin D. Roosevelt appoints William Hastie as the first Black federal judge over the U.S. Virgin Islands.

2008 The state of Florida apologizes for its sanctions of slavery during the pre-emancipation era.

 # MARCH 27

1909 Civil rights and peace activist African American Wally Nelson is born in Altheimer, Arkansas.

1921 With a career spanning over 65 years, African American dancer, actor, and choreographer Harold Nicholas is born in Winston-Salem, North Carolina.

1924 Dynamic award-winning jazz singer African American Sara Vaughn is born in Newark, New Jersey.

1934 Dancer, the first African American dancer with the New York city Ballet, and director of the Dance Theater of Harlem, Arthur Mitchell is born in New York, New York.

1944 Jesse Brown, the first African American Secretary of Veterans Affairs, is born in Detroit, Michigan.

1970 African American pop singer, songwriter, and producer Mariah Carey is born in Huntington, New York.

 # MARCH 28

1760 White influencial abolitionist in the emancipation of British slaves, Thomas Clarkson is born.

1878 Co-founder of the National Association for the Advancement of Colored People (NAACP), white Jewish-American Arthur Spingarn is born.

1939 All Black and African American owned basketball team, the New York Renaissance Big Five, won the first world championship of basketball.

1966 The first African American to be appointed head coach of a NBA team, Bill Russell, is named head coach of the Boston Celtics.

 # MARCH 29

1918 Singer, actress, special ambassador to the United Nations and Presidential Medal of Freedom recipient, Pearl Bailey is born in Newport News, Virginia.

JAN
FEB
MAR
APR
MAY
JUN
JUL
AUG
SEP
OCT
NOV
DEC

1924 The first African American to play for the New York Giants and the first African American inducted into the National Football League Hall of Fame, Emlen Tunnell is born.

1933 Highly regarded artist Eugene E. White is born in Ozan, Arkansas.

White opened the first art gallery in San Francisco owned by an African American.

1943 College administrator and the first African American sheriff in Florida since the Civil War, Nathaniel Glover is born in Jacksonville, Florida.

📑 MARCH 30

1870 The Fifteenth Amendment is ratified, making it illegal to deny any man the right to vote based on color.

1914 Blues harmonica player Sonny Boy Williamson is born in Madison County, Tennessee.

1964 The Supreme Court rules that all

citizens, regardless of race, are legally entitled to customary forms of polite social address in Hamilton v. Alabama.

1964 Folk singer and song writer Tracy Chapman is born in Cleveland, Ohio.

2002 For the first time two African

American basketball coaches, Mike Davis, and Melvin Sampson, compete against each other in the NCAA Final Four.

 # MARCH 31

1797 Olaudah Equiano, slave, world traveler, abolitionist, and author dies at sea. Equiano's autobiography becomes a narrative that advances the cause of the abolition of slavery in England.

1817 The New York legislature makes New York the first state to completely abolish slavery.

1840 Freed slave and Civil War spy Mary Elizabeth Bowser is born in Virginia.

1878 The first African American heavyweight boxing champion, Jack Johnson is born in Galveston, Texas.

1942 Award-winning African American journalist Robert McGruder is born in Louisville, Kentucky. He was known for advocating for women and minorities in the field of journalism.

1969 The first African to be appointed minister in the Swedish government, Nyamko Sabuni is born. She held the office of Minister for Integration and Gender Equality.

JAN
FEB
MAR
APR
MAY
JUN
JUL
AUG
SEP
OCT
NOV
DEC

Booker T. Washington addressing a crowd from the porch of a small building in Brownsville, Texas, ca. 1900

 # APRIL 1

1854 One of the United States' first African American Catholic Priests, Augustus Tolton, is born in Ralls County, Missouri.

1868 The Hampton Normal and Agricultural Institute, later to become Hampton University, HBCU, is opened. Hampton counts Booker T. Washington as one of its most noted graduates.

1905 African American Clara Hale, known as Mother Hale in work with caring for children and troubled mothers, and founder of the Hale House in New York is born in Elizabeth City, North Carolina.

1911 Augusta Baker, African American librarian, and advocate for the realistic depiction of Black children in literature, is born is born in Baltimore, Maryland.

APRIL 2

1870 African American Dr. J. Edward Perry is born in Clarksville, Texas. Dr. Perry and his associates opened the Perry Sanitarium and Training School for Nurses in Kansas City.

1918 Charles White, African American social artist, is born in Chicago, Illinois.

1939 Celebrated African American R&B singer/song writer Marvin Gaye is born in Washington, D. C.

1984 John Thompson becomes the first African American basketball coach to win the NCAA championship.

2019 The first African American woman mayor of Chicago, Lori Lightfoot, is elected.

 # APRIL 3

1858 The first Black member of the Nebraska Legislature, Dr. Matthew Ricketts, is born in Henry County, Kentucky.

1944 The Supreme Court decides the case of Smith v Allwright, making it illegal to prevent any legal voter from participating in primary elections based on color.

JAN
FEB
MAR
APR
MAY
JUN
JUL
AUG
SEP
OCT
NOV
DEC

1963 In Birmingham, Alabama Martin Luther King, Jr. begins the civil rights campaign against discrimination.

1973 Leila Smith is elected the first African American woman mayor in the U. S. She is voted mayor of Taft Oklahoma.

1996 African American Commerce Secretary of the United States Ron Brown is killed in a plane crash in Dubrovnik, Croatia

 # APRIL 4

1792 Thaddeus Stevens, a white politician who fought tenaciously for the abolition of slavery, is born in Danville, Vermont

1872 Prominent African American artist, sculptor, and expert in ceramics, Isaac Scott Hathaway is born in Lexington, Kentucky.

1928 Award-winning African American author, actor, and civil rights advocate Maya Angelou is born in St. Louis, Missouri.

1968 Martin Luther King is assassinated in Memphis, Tennessee, sparking riots in at least 125 locations around the country.

APRIL 5

1824 Moses Dickson, African American Union soldier, minister, and conductor on the Underground Railroad, is born in Cincinnati, Ohio.

1839 African American Civil War Naval hero and South Carolina congressman, Robert Smalls is born in Beaufort, South Carolina.

1856 Influential African American leader, intellectual, and founder of the Tuskegee Institute, Booker T. Washington is born.

1915 Legendary African American basketball coach John McLendon is born.

1937 4-Star general and first African American secretary of state Colin Powel is born.

APRIL 6

1905 African American Doctor William Cardozo is born. Cardozo is known for his groundbreaking research on sickle cell anemia.

1909 African American Matthew Henson, along with Robert Peary, are the first to reach the North Pole.

1968 After a gunfight between Black Panthers and Oakland Police, Bobby Hutton is shot and killed by police as he attempts to surrender.

1996 The Rwandan genocide of the African Tutsis by Hutus begins in what will end as the extermination of over 500,000 people.

2013 In a first of its kind occurrence, African American brothers B. J. and Justin Upton of the Atlanta Braves hit back-to-back homeruns to beat the Chicago Cubs.

 # APRIL 7

1842 Former slave, minister, military officer, and organizer of Allensworth, California, a town for freed Blacks, Allen Allensworth is born in Louisville, Kentucky.

1885 African American Granville Woods receives his first patent of over 50 he would be awarded during his lifetime.

1907 Pittsburg Pirates (Steelers) founding member and acclaimed African American college football coach Ray Kemp is born Cecil, Pennsylvania.

1917 Iconic blues and jazz singer, African American Billie Holiday is born in Philadelphia, Pennsylvania.

APRIL 8

1909 Folk artist and creator of The Throne of the Third Haven of the Nation's Millennium General Assembly, James Hampton is born in Elloree, South Carolina.

1920 Prominent African American jazz singer and pianist Carmen McRae is born.

1938 Renowned Ghanaian diplomat and Nobel Peace Prize recipient Kofi Annan is born.

1970 Charles Gordone wins the first Pulitzer Prize for drama awarded to an African American.

1974 African American Hank Aaron hits his 715th home run, holding the all-time home run hitter record for 33 years.

 # APRIL 9

1816 The African Methodist Episcopal Church, the first independent African American church, is organized in Philadelphia, Pennsylvania.

1866 The United States Congress passes the Civil Rights Act of 1866, which declared all persons born in the U. S. citizens regardless of race or color, or prior slavery.

JAN
FEB
MAR
APR
MAY
JUN
JUL
AUG
SEP
OCT
NOV
DEC

APR

MAY
JUN
JUL
AUG
SEP
OCT
NOV

DEC

1914 Noted African American author and educator Ralph Ellison is born in Oklahoma City, Oklahoma.

1939 African American Marian Anderson sings in front of the Lincoln Memorial in Washington, D.C. as when she refused to sing at Constitution Hall, which prevented integrated audiences from attending.

1898 Professional football player, lawyer and singer, Paul Robeson is born in Princeton, New Jersey. Robeson was the first African American at Rutgers University.

 ## APRIL 10

1887 African American chemist Edward Chandler, known for his work with carbon compounds, is born in Ocala, Florida.

1914 Innovative African American gospel music composer, Noah Ryder is born in Nashville, Tennessee.

1947 Jackie Robinson, the first African American major league baseball player, signs with the Brooklyn Dodgers.

1963 Accomplished African American poet Reginald Shepherd is born in New York, New York.

1981 Racial tensions explode in London starting England's Brixton Riot. After 3 days of rioting as many as 300 people were injured and caused an estimated $8.8 million in damage.

JAN
FEB
MAR
APR
MAY
JUN
JUL
AUG
SEP
OCT
NOV
DEC

 ## APRIL 11

145 Septimius Severus, North African Roman emperor, is born in Leptis Magna, Libya.

1881 Atlanta Baptist Female Seminary, later to become HBCU Spelman College, is established by Sophia B. Packard and Harriet E. Giles.

1899 Percy Julian, an African American pioneer in pharmaceutical research and development, is born Montgomery, Alabama.

1908 The first African American woman judge in the United States, Jane Bolin is born in Poughkeepsie, New York.

1966 Emmett Ashford becomes the first African American umpire in major league baseball.

 ## APRIL 12

1861 The American Civil War begins with the Battle of Fort Sumter in Charleston Harbor.

1864 Confederate troops gun down approximately 300 Black Union soldiers in what has become known as the Fort Pillow Massacre.

1787 The Free African Society

JAN
FEB
MAR
APR
MAY
JUN
JUL
AUG
SEP
OCT
NOV
DEC

is established in Philadelphia, Pennsylvania by Richard Allen, and Absalom Jones.

1909 Influential African American jazz musician and band leader Lionel Hampton is born in Louisville, Kentucky.

1983 Harold Washington wins the election for mayor of Chicago, becoming the city's first African American Mayor.

 # APRIL 13

1873 Between 60 and 140 African Americans are murdered in the Colfax Massacre. An attack by white supremacists threatened by the political involvement of the newly freed Blacks.

1924 African American mural artist John Biggers is born in Gastonia, North Carolina.

1954 Curt Roberts becomes the first African American to play for the Pittsburgh Pirates baseball team.

1963 Sidney Poitier wins the Best Male Actor Oscar for his role in *Lilies of the Field*. He is the first African American to win the award.

1997 Tiger Woods becomes the first African American and the youngest to win the Masters Tournament.

2003 Outstanding African American basketball great

Michael Jordan retires for the third, and final time, from professional basketball.

Tiger Woods at the World Golf Championship in Miami, Florida, in February 2007

 # APRIL 14

1775 A group of Quakers forms The Society for the Relief of Free Negroes Unlawfully Held in Bondage, Abolition Society in America, in Philadelphia, Pennsylvania.

....

1824 The site for Fort Scott Kansas is chosen by Captain B. D. Moore. The Colored Volunteer Infantry were stationed there to help keep the peace between Native Americans and the white settlers.

....

1897 Voorhees College is established by 23-year-old Elizabeth Evelyn Wright in Denmark, South Carolina. An HBCU, it is associated with the Episcopal Church and accredited by the Southern Association of Colleges and Schools.

....

JAN
FEB
MAR
APR
MAY
JUN
JUL
AUG
SEP
OCT
NOV
DEC

1925 African American swing-era saxophonist Gene Ammons is born in Chicago, Illinois.

1954 Contemporary African American poet Cornelius Eady is born in Rochester, New York.

1955 Elston Howard plays his first game for the New York Yankees, the first Black player to play for the Yankees.

2002 Tiger Woods wins his 3rd Masters Golf title.

 # APRIL 15

1889 Prominent African American leader of the American Civil Rights movement and union organizer, A. Philip Randolph is born in Crescent City, Florida.

1919 African American playwright Loften Mitchel is born in Columbus, North Carolina.

1928 The first licensed African American woman architect in the United States, Norma Sklarek, is born in Harlem, New York.

1947 Playing for the Brooklyn Dodgers, Jackie Robinson becomes the first African American to play in a professional baseball game.

1960 Student Non-violent Coordinating Committee begins in Raleigh, North Carolina with the help of civil rights activist Ella Baker.

APRIL 16

1862 President Abraham Lincoln signs an act ending slavery in Washington, D. C.

1864 Medical missionary to Africa and the first African American woman doctor licensed to practice medicine in Tennessee Georgia Patton Washington is born in Grundy County, Tennessee.

1929 The first African American woman to earn a Ph.D. in chemistry, Marie Daly, is born Corona, New York.

1947 African American basketball legend Kareem Abdul-Jabbar is born in New York, New York.

 # APRIL 17

1843 Theophilus Steward, intellectual and one of the organizers of the AME Church is born in Gouldtown, New Jersey.

1863 Charlotte L. Brown is removed from a San Francisco streetcar leading to the civil rights case that initiated the right of Blacks to ride streetcars in California.

1912 Teacher and integral organizer of

JAN
FEB
MAR
APR
MAY
JUN
JUL
AUG
SEP
OCT
NOV
DEC

the Montgomery Bus Boycott, Jo Ann Gibson Robinson is born Culloden, Georgia.

1823 Entrepreneur and first elected African American Judge Mifflin Gibbs is born in Philadelphia, Pennsylvania.

1980 Rhodesia gains permanent independence from Brittan and becomes the South African country of Zimbabwe.

 APRIL 18

1813 The first formally educated African American medical doctor, James McCune Smith is born in New York, New York. Smith trained to Glasgow, Scotland to receive his medical degree, due to racism in the U. S.

1922 African American heavyweight boxer, Jack Johnson, receives patent for a wrench.

1925 African American Beat poet Bob Kaufman is born in New Orleans, Louisiana.

1926 The first African American to be drafted by an NFL team, Wallace Triplett is born in La Mott, Pennsylvania.

1950 Sam Jethroe is traded by the Brooklyn Dodgers to become the first African American on the Boston Braves.

1966 Bill Russell is named head coach of the Boston Celtics,

making him the first
African American

professional basketball
coach.

 ## APRIL 19

1775 The beginnings
of the Revolutionary
War at Lexington and
Concord are fought by
the Minutemen and
included free Blacks.

1841 African
American Pierre
Landry, politician,
minister, and lawyer
is born in Ascension
Parish, Louisiana.

1866 President
Andrew Johnson
delivers a speech to
4,000-5,000 people in

Washington. D. C. to
celebrate the abolition
of slavery.

1887 The patent for
Lubricator Attachment
for steam locomotives
is granted to African
American Elijah
McCoy.

1914 Politician Cora
M. Brown is born in
Bessemer, Alabama.
She becomes the first
African American
woman to be elected to
the state senate.

 ## APRIL 20

1899 Harlem
Renaissance artist
Ellis Wilson is born in
Mayfield, Kentucky.

1909 Everett Fredrick
Morrow, Administrative
Officer for Special
Projects to President

Dwight D. Eisenhower, is born; the first African American to hold an executive position on a president's staff.

1912 Noted church architect Lester Bankhead is born is Union, South Carolina.

1951 Popular African American soul singer of the 1970s and 80s Luther Vandross is born in New York, New York.

1986 African American basketball legend Michael Jordan sets record 63 points in the playoff games.

 # APRIL 21

1878 The Liberian Exodus, a 42-day journey carrying 206 African Americans to Liberia to escape the difficulties in the United States, leaves Charleston South Carolina.

1883 Noted African American architect Clarence Wigington is born in Lawrence, Kansas.

1884 Robert Reyburn forms the first Black medical association, Medic-Chirugical Society of the District of Columbia.

1906 The first African American woman certified public accountant (CPA), Mary Washington Wylie is born in Vicksburg, Mississippi.

1910 The National Urban League is

founded in New York, New York, with George Haynes as President.

2018 Colin Kaepernick, African American football player and activist, is awarded Amnesty International's Ambassador of Conscience Award.

 APRIL 22

1882 Notable African American author and educator Benjamin Brawley is born in Columbia, South Carolina.

1891 Original Delta Blues musician African American Charley Patton is born in Bolton, Mississippi.

1922 Jazz bassist and composer Charles Mingus is born in Los Angeles, California. Mingus' collaborations in jazz included Louis Armstrong, Lionel Hampton, Duke Ellington, and Miles Davis.

1933 African American Civil rights and labor activist Norman Hill is born in Summit, New Jersey.

1947 Radio station executive and owner African American Catherine (Woods) Hughes is born in Omaha, Nebraska.

 APRIL 23

JAN FEB MAR APR MAY JUN JUL AUG SEP OCT NOV DEC

A postage stamp showing an image of Charles Mingus, circa 1995

COMPOSER AND BASSIST

32 USA

CHARLES

1856 Inventor Granville T. Woods, holder of over 50 patents, most notably the Multiplex Railway Telegraph, is born in Columbus, Ohio.

1872 Charlotte E. Ray becomes the first Black woman to practice law in the United States.

1895 African American clarinet player Jimmie Noone, an early jazz player and music conductor who bridged into swing jazz, is born in Cut Off, Louisiana.

1951 Sixteen-year-old Barbara Johns leads a protest that begins a 2-week strike of over-crowded Moton High School in Farmville, Virginia. This action resulted in NAACP filing suit, and a Supreme Court ruling that the school board must integrate its schools.

2015 Loretta Lynch is confirmed by the United States Senate as the first African American woman to hold the position of Attorney General.

 APRIL 24

1898 Spain declares war on the United States beginning the Spanish American War. Over 3,000 African American soldiers were some of the first to take part in this military conflict.

1919 South Carolina creates Emmett Scott High School in Rock Hill; its first school for Blacks.

1919 Influential African American mathematician and game theory expert David Blackwell is born in Centralia, Illinois.

1937 African American Joe Henderson, renowned jazz saxophonist, was born in Lima, Ohio.

1954 Radical African American social activist and writer Mumia Abu-Jamal is born in Philadelphia, Pennsylvania.

 # APRIL 25

1872 Influential and innovative African American social worker Minnie Crosthwaite is born in Nashville, Tennessee.

1917 One of the most significant singers of the 20th century, Ella Fitzgerald is born in Newport News, Virginia. Fitzgerald was the first African American woman to win a Grammy Award.

1917 White, Jewish mother and education equality activist Esther Brown is born Kansas City, Missouri.

1942 Rubye Smith Robinson, civil rights activist, is born in Atlanta, Georgia.

1944 The United Negro College Fund is organized to provide monetary assistance to disadvantaged students.

 ## APRIL 26

1792 Free-born African American John Vashon, businessman, seaman, and abolitionist is born in Norfolk, Virginia.

1798 African and Crow Native American trapper, explorer and fur trader, Joe Beckwourth is born in Frederick County, Virginia.

1869 African American William T. Francis, lawyer, and minister to Liberia, is born in Indianapolis, Indiana.

1892 The patent for the invention of the ironing board is granted to African American Sarah Boone.

1886 "Mother of the Blues," professional African American blues singer Ma Rainey is born in Columbus, Georgia.

1886 William Dawson, influential politician and the first African American to head a regular Congressional committee is born in Anniston, Alabama.

1994 South Africa has its first all-race elections where Nelson

Mandela is elected
president.

 ## APRIL 27

President
Ronald
Reagan shakes
hands with
Coretta Scott
King in 1983

1883 Writer and
activist Hubert
Harrison is born in
St. Croix, U. S. Virgin
Islands. Harrison
actively fought against
the subservient
stereotypes of Blacks
during that time.

1903 African
American W.E.B. DuBois
publishes his influential
book of essays, *The
Souls of Black Folk.*

1926 Lawyer,
politician and first
African American
New York Secretary of
State, Basil Alexander
Paterson is born in
Harlem, New York.

1927 The wife of
Martin Luther King,
Jr. and powerful civil
rights activist in her
own right, Coretta
Scott King is born
Heiberger, Alabama.

1945 Two-time
Pulitzer Prize-winning
African American
playwright August

Wilson is born in Pittsburgh, Pennsylvania.

2007 Barbara Hillary, age 75, becomes the first Black woman to reach the North Pole.

 APRIL 28

1846 Former slave turned congressman; Jeremiah Haralson is born outside Columbus, Ohio.

1874 African American vaudeville performer, Belle Davis is born in Chicago, Illinois.

1891 The patent for a ship's propeller is awarded to African American George Toliver.

1901 WWI "Harlem Hellfighter" Needham Roberts is born in Trenton, New Jersey. Roberts and fellow

Hellfighter Henry Johnson received the French Croix de Guerre medal; the only Americans to do so.

1922 Lawyer, civil rights supporter and founding member of the Congress of Racial Equality, African American Jewel Stradford is born in Chicago, Illinois.

1967 Muhammad Ali is stripped of his World Heavyweight Boxing title due to his refusal to be drafted into the military on the grounds of being a conscientious objector.

 APRIL 29

1845 Macon B. Allen and Robert Morris, Jr. become partners in the first Black law practice in the U. S.

1854 The Ashmun Institute, the first college for blacks, receives its charter in Oxford, Pennsylvania. It later becomes Lincoln University, an HBCU.

1899 World-renowned musician, band leader, and composer Duke Ellington is born in Washington, D. C. Ellington was one of the creators of the popular "big-band" style of music.

1922 Parren Mitchel, the first African American Congressman from Maryland and founding member of the Congressional Black Caucus, is born in Baltimore, Maryland.

1945 Popular 1960s African American R&B singer Tammi Terrell is born in Philadelphia, Pennsylvania. She was noted for her duets with singing legend Marvin Gaye.

1947 Renowned and prolific African American poet Yusef Komunyakaa is born in Bogalusa, Louisiana.

1992 The L. A. Race Riots begin after a not guilty verdict for police officers accused of unnecessary force in the beating of Rodney King.

 APRIL 30

JAN
FEB
MAR
APR
MAY
JUN
JUL
AUG
SEP
OCT
NOV
DEC

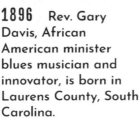

Los Angeles police officers in riot gear advance past a burning police car on night one of the Rodney King Riots on April 29, 1992

1896   Rev. Gary Davis, African American minister blues musician and innovator, is born in Laurens County, South Carolina.

1900   On the day of Casey Jones' death, Wallace Saunders writes the folk song, "The Ballad of Casey Jones."

1920   African American cosmetologist and health activist Odessa Brown is born in Des Arc, Arkansas.

1926   The first African American woman pilot, Bessie Coleman, dies in a plane crash due to mechanical difficulties.

1941   R&B and jazz singer, African American Shirley Witherspoon is born in Minneapolis, Minnesota.

MAY 1

1875 The Huntsville Normal School begins classes with 61 students. Huntsville Normal School eventually becomes Alabama A&M University, an HBCU.

1901 Sterling Allen Brown, prominent Afro-American poet, and teacher, is born in Washington, D. C.

1915 Gold medal winner of the 400-meter track event at the 1936 Olympics, Air Force pilot, and teacher, African American Archie Williams is born in Oakland, California.

1930 One of the first inductees into the Blues Hall of Fame, African American Little Walter, harmonica luminary is born in Marksville, Louisiana.

1939 The first African American network news anchor Max Robinson was born in Richmond, Virginia.

1950 Gwendolyn Brooks, author, and poet, receives the first Pulitzer Prize awarded to an African American.

1951 The Chicago White Sox become integrated by signing Negro League baseball player, Orestes Miñoso.

JAN FEB MAR APR MAY JUN JUL AUG SEP OCT NOV DEC

MAY 2

1762 The first African American doctor in the U. S., James Derham, is born in Philadelphia, Pennsylvania.

1844 Black inventor Elijah McCoy is born in Colchester, Canada. His inventions contributed to the improvements to the steam engine.

1879 African American social activist and teacher, Nannie Burroughs is born in Orange, Virginia.

1920 The National Negro Baseball League plays its first game.

1936 The Ethiopian Emperor, Haile Selassie, goes into exile due to Italian invasion into Ethiopia.

1963 The week-long "Children's Crusade" in Birmingham, Alabama begins. It ends a week later with concessions for desegregated lunch counters, businesses, and restrooms. Over 2,000 children ages 7-18 participated in the crusade.

 # MAY 3

1876 A riot breaks out in Indianapolis, Indiana on election day between Blacks who were trying to vote and whites who were trying to intimidate them to keep them from doing so.

1898 Educational activist and pioneer in adult education, African American Septima Clark is born in Charleston, South Carolina.

1920 Master African American jazz pianist and composer, John Lewis is born in La Grange, Illinois. Lewis was part of the iconic Modern Jazz Quartet.

1921 African American Heavyweight Boxing Champion and legend Sugar Ray Robinson is born in Ailey, Georgia.

1933 James Brown, African American singing super star and considered by many as the "Godfather of Soul," is born in Barnwell, South Carolina.

1948 The Supreme Court rules in the case of Shelley v. Kramer, that the restrictive sale of property to non-Caucasians violates the equal protection clause of the 14th Amendment.

 ## MAY 4

1848 African American newspaper publisher and politician, John Quincy Adams is born. (This is not President John Quincy Adams.)

1860 Doctor, writer and co-founder of the Ohio Mutual Medical Association, Thomas William Burton is born in Madison County, Kentucky.

1891 The first Black owned hospital, Provident Hospital and Training School, is

opened by Dr. Daniel Williams, on Chicago's South side.

1897 Joseph H. Smith, an African American, is granted a patent for a rotary head lawn sprinkler.

1941 African American singer and songwriter, Nick Ashford is born in Fairfield, South Carolina. Ashford and co-writer Valarie Simpson wrote songs for Ray Charles, Aretha Franklin, Ronnie Milsap and Marvin Gaye and Tammi Terrell.

1961 Freedom Rides begin on buses from Washington, D. C. to the South to encourage enforcement of the Supreme Court's ruling of desegregation of interstate bus lines.

MAY 5

1808 Governor of California under Mexican rule, Pio Pico, African, Native American, and European, is born in Mission San Gabriel.

1865 Adam Clayton Powell, pastor and one of the founders of the National Urban League, is born in Franklin County, Virginia.

1919 The National Conference on Lynching takes place in New York City to gain public support of the Dyer Anti-Lynching Bill. The bill was defeated.

1905 Robert S. Abbott becomes the publisher of the

Chicago Defender, which goes on to become the largest newspaper of African American interest at that time.

1938 Chart-topping African American R&B singer, Johnnie Taylor is born in Crawfordsville, Arkansas. Taylor's most memorable song is "Disco Lady."

1950 A collection of poetry, *Annie Allen,* by Gwendolyn Brooks receives the first Pulitzer Prize awarded to an African American.

 ## MAY 6

1787 The first African American Masonic Lodge is established in Boston.

1812 Martin R. Delany is born a free person of color in Charles Town, Virginia. Delany was a vocal proponent for black nationalism.

1864 Traveling African American preacher and poet, Lena Mason is born in Quincy, Illinois.

1905 Police officer, teacher and politician, African American Leon Jordan is born in Kansas City, Missouri. Jordan served in the Missouri House of Representatives from 1964-1970.

1931 Legendary African American baseball player and homerun king Willie Mays is born in Westfield, Alabama.

1938 The Works Progress

Administration is created by President Franklin Delano Roosevelt to aid in the employment of many who were affected by the flagging economy of the Great Depression.

1960 President Dwight D. Eisenhower signs the Civil Rights Act of 1960.

MAY 7

1700 Quaker William Penn begins meetings to help blacks advocate for emancipation.

1845 The first African American nurse, Mary Mahoney is born in Boston, Massachusetts.

1888 African American poet, playwright and author, Fenton Johnson was born in Chicago, Illinois.

1910 Civil rights activist and prominent African American doctor in Broward County, Florida, Von Mizell is born in Fort Lauderdale, Florida.

1911 Lawyer William Ming Jr. is born in Chicago Illinois. Ming was a on the legal team in the landmark case of Brown v. Board of Education.

1943 The liberty ship SS George Washington Carver is launched. The ship is named to honor African American agricultural scientist George Washington Carver.

A parade celebrating the 11th anniversary of the Brotherhood of Sleeping Car Porters Union in New York City, 1936

JAN
FEB
MAR
APR
MAY
JUN
JUL
AUG
SEP
OCT
NOV
DEC

 # MAY 8

1753 Phyllis Wheatley a Black slave and international author is born in Senegambia, Africa.

1866 The first African American to graduate from the University of Minnesota Law School and the first African American to be elected to the Minnesota House of Representatives, John Francis Wheaton is born in Hagerstown, Maryland.

1902 Fay Jackson, founder of *Flash* magazine, the west coast's first black magazine, is born in Dallas, Texas.

1925 The Brotherhood of Sleeping Car Porters is organized by Philip Randolph to help protect the employment rights of African American railcar workers.

1932 African American heavyweight boxer who had 39

JAN
FEB
MAR
APR
MAY
JUN
JUL
AUG
SEP
OCT
NOV
DEC

career knockouts, Sonny Liston is born in Sand Slough, Arkansas.

. . . .

1958 African American Lovie Smith

high school, college and professional football coach is born in Gladewater, Texas.

. . . .

 ## MAY 9

1897 Forward thinking African American doctor, music arranger, poet and writer, Rudolph Fisher is born in Washington, D. C.

. . . .

1899 John Albert Burr receives a patent for his rotary lawn mower.

. . . .

1939 African American 1960 Olympic

track and field gold-medalist Ralph Boston is born in Laurel, Mississippi.

. . . .

1960 Tony Gwynn, African American baseball player and hitting phenomenon, is born in Los, Angeles California. Gwynn played professional baseball for 20 years, all for the San Diego Padres.

. . . .

 ## MAY 10

1775 In a precursor to the Revolutionary War, Blacks help in

the capture of Fort Ticonderoga.

. . . .

1815 Escaped slave, author of *Narrative of the Life and Adventures of Henry Bibb,* and editor of Canada's first Black newspaper, *Voice of the Fugitive,* Henry Bibb is born on a plantation in Kentucky.

. . . .

1837 Civil War officer and first African American governor in the U. S., Pickney Pinchback, is born in Macon, Georgia.

. . . .

1902 White, Jewish rabbi, civil rights activist, and speaker on the 1963 March on Washington, Joachim Prinz, is born in Prussia.

. . . .

1994 South Africa's first Black president and activist, Nelson Mandela, is inaugurated.

. . . .

 # MAY 11

1834 African American Civil War correspondent, lawyer, and superintendent of education Thomas Morris Chester is born in Harrisburg, Pennsylvania.

. . . .

1885 One of the innovators of Dixieland style jazz and teacher of trumpet player Louis Armstrong, African American King Oliver is born in Aben, Louisiana.

. . . .

1892 African American jockey Alonzo Clayton becomes the youngest rider to win the Kentucky Derby. He still holds the title today.

. . . .

1933 Influential African American Muslim leader Louis Farrakhan is born in New York, New York.

1968 The Poor People's Campaign begins across the United States, to bring attention to the plight of the nation's poor blacks, whites, Native Americans, and Hispanics.

A record titled *An Evening with Louis Armstrong and All His Stars at the Pasadena Civic Auditorium* from Crescendo Record Co. Inc., 1977

 MAY 12

1862 Deckhand Robert Smalls escapes slavery by seizing the Confederate ship, the "Planter," and sails it out of Charleston Harbor and delivering it to the Union Navy.

1883 African American teacher and one of the leading pianist of her time, Hazel Harrison is born in Le Porte, Indiana.

1916 Black social writer and critic Albert Murray is born in Nokomis, Alabama.

1926 Mervyn Dymally, African American politician, teacher, and immigrant is born in Trinidad in the British West Indies.

1955 Sam Jones of the Chicago Cubs becomes the first African American baseball pitcher to throw a no-hitter.

MAY 13

1871 The oldest historically black land grant college, Alcorn University, is incorporated in Mississippi.

1872 Matilda Evans, the first African American woman to receive her medical practitioner's license in South Carolina, is born.

1888 Slavery is ended in Brazil by Princess Isabel.

1914 Great African American heavyweight boxer Joe Louis is born Lafayette, Alabama.

1933 African American Dodgers' catcher John Roseboro is born in Ashland, Ohio. Roseboro played in 4 World Series games.

1950 Legendary recording artist and 25-time Grammy award winner Stevie Wonder is born in Saginaw, Michigan.

JAN
FEB
MAR
APR
MAY
JUN
JUL
AUG
SEP
OCT
NOV
DEC

MAY 14

1781 African slave, engineer, and Russian general, Abram Petrovich Hannibal, dies in St. Petersburg, Russia. He is the great-grandfather of the famous Russian writer, Alexander Pushkin.

1888 Construction engineer and one-time governor of the Virgin Islands, Archie Alexander is born in Ottumwa, Iowa.

1897 Improvisational African American jazz saxophonist Sidney Bechet is born in New Orleans, Louisiana.

1898 Innovative jazz drummer Zutty Singleton is born in Bunkie, Louisiana.

1927 African Canadian sculptor and portrait artist, Artis Lane is born in Ontario. She painted portraits of such notable people as, Michael Jordan and Nelson Mandela.

1963 Noted tennis pro Arthur Ashe becomes the first African American to make the U. S. Davis Cup team.

 # MAY 15

1891 The Delaware General Assembly establishes the Delaware College for Colored Students, which is to become Delaware State University an HBCU.

1919 Mary Charles, Prime Minister of the Island of Dominica is born in Port Michael.

1934 Prominent psychiatrist Alvin Poussaint is born in Harlem, New York.

2002 Bobby Cherry is convicted of the Alabama church bombing in which four Black children were killed on September 15, 1963, and sentenced to life in prison.

2002 Due to the efforts of African American Marsha Coleman-Adebayo, President George W. Bush signs the Notification and Federal employee Anti-discrimination and Retaliation Act (the No FEAR Act).

 # MAY 16

1792 The slave trade in Denmark is abolished.

1887 Renowned African American artist and teacher Laura Waring is born in Hartford, Connecticut.

1929 U.S. Congressman from Michigan for 52 years, African American John Conyers, Jr. is born in Detroit, Michigan.

1950 The civil rights case of Briggs v. Elliot is filed in U. S. District Court. The ruling was that the schools must be "equalized," but not integrated.

1976 Asa Philip Randolph, Civil Rights, and labor activist, dies in New York, New York.

JAN
FEB
MAR
APR
MAY
JUN
JUL
AUG
SEP
OCT
NOV
DEC

1875 Oliver Lewis is the African American jockey to win the first Kentucky Derby.

1892 African American inventor of refrigeration and automobile improvements and racecar driver, Frederick McKinley Jones is born in Covington, Kentucky.

1903 One of the fastest men in the Negro Baseball League, James Bell, known to fans as Cool Papa, is born in Starkville, Mississippi.

1929 African American author of 48 children's books and poet Eloise Greenfield is born in Parmele, North Carolina.

1954 The Supreme Court overturns legal school segregation in Brown v. Board of Education of Topeka, Kansas.

1980 Miami Riot is spurred by the acquittal of four police officers for beating Arthur McDuffie to death. McDuffie's family settled a civic suit against Dade County for $1.1 million in 1981.

MAY 18

1896 The Supreme Court upholds the concept of "separate, but equal" in the case of Plessy v. Ferguson.

1911 Big Joe Turner, the African American singer who bridged the transition from Blues to Rock and Roll, is born in Kansas City, Missouri.

1912 South African politician and activist Walter Sisulu is born in the village of Qutubeni, South Africa.

MAY 19

1744 Sophie Charlotte future Queen of England is born. She is the second Black queen of England, a descendant of the African line of royals from Portugal.

1894 Seattle, Washington's first African American newspaper, The Seattle Republican is published.

1946 Baseball legend and civil rights activist Reggie Jackson is born in Wyncote. Pennsylvania.

1960 Top-ranked Black French tennis player and singer Yannick Noah, is born in Sedan, France.

1925 Charismatic political activist and Black Nationalist Malcom X is born in Omaha, Nebraska.

1930 Author of A Raisin in the Sun, the first Broadway play written by an African American woman, Lorraine Hansberry is born in Chicago, Illinois.

1950 Olympic hurdles gold medalist,

Rod Milburn is born in Opelousas, Louisiana.

1976 Professional basketball player and

NBA Hall of Fame inductee, Kevin Garnett is born in Mauldin, South Carolina.

 MAY 20

1862 U.S. Congress passes the Homestead Act which allowed any adult head of household up to 160 acres of land for a nominal filing fee.

1899 Influential Afro Cuban author, Lydia

Cabrera is born in Havana, Cuba.

1954 The first African American Governor of New York, David Paterson, is born. He is also the second legally blind person to serve in that capacity.

 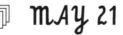 MAY 21

1862 President Abraham Lincoln establishes public schools for African American children in Washington. D. C.

1901 African American librarian, playwright, and

supporter of the Harlem Renaissance, Regina Anderson is born in Chicago, Illinois.

1904 Legendary African American jazz pianist and entertainer

Fats Waller is born in Harlem, New York.

1923 Gospel singer, songwriter, and choir director, African American Doris Akers is born in Brookfield, Missouri.

1924 One of the winningest college basketball coaches in history African American Clarence Gains is born in Paducah, Kentucky. Gains served as coach of Winston-Salem University's Rams for 47 years.

1969 The Greensboro Uprising at Dudley High School and North Carolina A&T University involving university and high school students, and over 600 National Guard troops.

 # MAY 22

1863 The Bureau of Colored Troops is formed by War Department General Order 143, to establish regiments of African American soldiers.

1940 African American broadcast journalist for CNN Bernard Shaw is born in Chicago, Illinois.

1941 Award-winning African American stage, screen and TV actor Paul Winfield is born in Los Angeles. His most notable role was in the lead character in the movie *Sounder*.

1966 The Emmy Awards present the first Best Actor in a Series Award to an African American.

MAY 23

1900 William Carney becomes the first African American to receive the Medal of Honor for his service in the Union Army during the Civil War.

1910 Enduring African American actor, singer and entertainer, Scatman Crothers is born in Terre Haute, Indianna.

1921 "Shuffle Along," a play written, directed, and acted by African Americans, debuts on Broadway.

1946 The first African American identical quadruplets, the Fultz Quadruplets, are born in the U.S.

1954 African American Marvin Hagler, middle weight boxing champion, is born.

1982 Lee P. Brown is named the first Black police commissioner of Houston, Texas.

 # MAY 24

1916 Lincoln Motion Pictures, the first African American owned film studio, is established.

1918 The first African American mayor of Detroit, Michigan, Coleman Young is born in Tuscaloosa, Alabama.

1935 Valerie Capers, blind African American jazz and classical pianist is born in New York, New York.

1967 Influencial Black rapper Heavy D is born in Mandeville, Jamaica.

 ## MAY 25

1878 African American Vaudeville dancer and performer Bill "Bojangles" Robinson is born.

1889 African American social advocate and president of the Baltimore NAACP chapter for 35 years, Lillie M. Carroll is born in Baltimore, Maryland.

1905 The first African American woman to receive her master's degree in library science, Dorothy Porter Wesley is born in Warrenton, Virginia.

1972 In an event to exhibit solidarity between African Americans and Africans around the world, the first African Liberation Day is held in Washington, D.C.

2020 African American George Floyd is killed by police in Minneapolis, Minnesota.

JAN
FEB
MAR
APR
MAY
JUN
JUL
AUG
SEP
OCT
NOV
DEC

MAY 26

1891 African American vaudeville entertainer Mamie Smith is born in Cincinnati, Ohio.

1899 Influential Harlem Renaissance painter, Aaron Douglas is born in Topeka, Kansas.

1913 Celebrated Black artist Gwendolyn Knight is born in Bridgetown, Barbados.

1926 African American Miles Davis, pioneering jazz trumpet virtuoso and composer, is born in Alton, Illinois.

1956 Althea Gibson becomes the first African American to win a major tennis tournament.

1965 The Voting Rights Act is passed by the U. S. Senate.

 # MAY 27

1849 Tom Wiggins Bethune, blind pianist, and composer is born in Columbus, Georgia.

1861 Former slave and self-educated journalist and social reformer, Victoria E.

Matthews is born in Fort Valley, Georgia.

1890 Librarian and historian Vivian Harsh is born. Harsh is credited with preserving and

curating Black history of the Chicago area.

1898 African American inventor and engineer of heating and cooling systems, David Crosthwait is born in Nashville, Tennessee.

1932 Versatile African American

blues, rockabilly, and R&B singer Junior Parker is born in Clarksdale, Mississippi.

1958 The first integrated African American student at Little Rock High School, Ernest Green, graduates.

 # MAY 28

1888 Radical political activist and founder of the magazine, The New Negro Movement, Cyril Briggs is born in Nevis, West Indies.

1898 African American band leader and musician, Andy Kirk is born in Newport, Kentucky.

1831 Eliza A. Gardner, religious leader, and social

activist is born in New York, New York.

1936 Social activist and administrator, African American Betty Shabazz is born in Detroit, Michigan. Shabazz is the widow of civil rights leader Malcom X.

2000 More than 200,000 protestors marched in Sydney, Australia for native Aboriginal rights.

2007 Parren Mitchel, the first African American Congressman from Maryland and founding member of the Congressional Black Caucus, dies in Baltimore, Maryland.

The Women's Rights Pioneers monument on The Mall in Central Park, New York City, featuring Sojourner Truth

MAY 29

1851 Abolitionist and women's rights activist Sojourner Truth gives her "Ain't I a Woman" speech.

1910 Ralph Metcalf, an African American member of the gold medal 1936 100-meter relay team, is born in Atlanta, Georgia.

1914 African American research scientist, chemist, and educator Henry McBay is born in Mexia, Texas

1947 Renowned and prolific African American poet Yusef Komunyakaa is born in Bogalusa, Louisiana.

1962 John O'Neil becomes the first African American professional baseball coach as manager of the Chicago Cubs.

1973 The first black mayor of Los Angeles, Thomas Bradley, is elected. He served as mayor for 20 years.

 ## MAY 30

1822 Denmark Vesey's planned rebellion is revealed and thwarted by authorities in Charleston, South Carolina.

1854 The Kansas-Nebraska Act, which allowed the territories of Kansas and Nebraska to decide on the issue of slavery by vote. At the time neither African Americans nor women could vote.

1881 The first African American to graduate from the Pennsylvania School of Fine arts and Architecture, architect Julian Abele is born in Philadelphia, Pennsylvania.

1903 Member of the Harlem Renaissance Society and poet Countee Cullen is born.

1915 Henry Hill, African American chemist, and expert in polymers, is born in St. Joseph, North Carolina.

1943 Civil rights worker James Chaney is born. Chaney was one of three workers killed in 1964 in Mississippi while promoting voting registration for Blacks.

MAY 31

1870 The Enforcement Act of 1870 was established to protect the rights of African Americans where there was open intimidation to keep Blacks from voting or running for office.

1909 The first conference of the National Negro Committee, latter to be the National Association for the Advancement of Colored People (NAACP) is held in New York.

1921 Tulsa Race Massacre begins. Within 24 hours 35 city blocks were burned to the ground and it is estimated up to 300 people lost their lives.

1924 Patricia Roberts Harris, the first female African American to serve as an ambassador and first African American woman to serve in a presidential cabinet position, is born in Mattoon, Illinois.

1931 World-renowned African American opera singer Shirley Verrett is born in New Orleans, Louisiana.

1945 A member of the Los Angeles Lakers from 1969-1974, Harold "Happy" Hairston is born in Winston-Salem, North Carolina.

Morgan Freeman at the 16th Annual SeaChange Summer Party on July 22, 2023, in Dana Point, California

 # JUNE 1

1849 African American suffragist and integration advocate, Virginia Hewlett Douglass is born in Cambridge, Massachusetts.

1876 African American Thomas Jefferson Huddleston, Sr. entrepreneur of funeral homes and founder of the Afro American Sons and Daughters Hospital in Yazoo City, Mississippi is born.

1937 African American Oscar winner for *Million Dollar Baby* and one of the most distinctive voices in entertainment, Morgan Freeman is born in Memphis, Tennessee.

1939 African American Howard Dodson, historian, and Director of the Schomburg Center for Research in Black Culture, is born in Chester, Pennsylvania.

1942 Alfred Masters becomes the first

JAN
FEB
MAR
APR
MAY
JUN
JUL
AUG
SEP
OCT
NOV
DEC

African American U. S. Marine since the Revolutionary War.

1994 South Africa rejoins the African Commonwealth of Nations after 33 years due to Apartheid.

 # JUNE 2

1854 Runaway slave, Anthony Burns, is reunited with his master in accordance with the Fugitive Slave Act. However, a Black church raises the $1300 to buy his freedom, less than a year later.

1863 Harriet Tubman leads Union Army soldiers to the Combahee River and rescues over 700 enslaved people.

1868 Educational advocate and leader African American John Hope is born in Augusta, Georgia.

1905 African American singer and musician, Valaida Snow is born in Cleveland City, Tennessee.

1907 Dorothy West, prominent African American writer from the Harlem Renaissance is born in Boston, Massachusetts.

1913 The New York state legislature passes a bill forming the 15th New York National Guard regiment. This group goes on to be known as the highly regarded Harlem Hellfighters.

JUNE 3

JAN
FEB
MAR
APR
MAY
JUN
JUL
AUG
SEP
OCT
NOV
DEC

1904 Medical pioneer and researcher of blood donations Dr. Charles Richard Drew is born in Washington, D.C.

1906 International African American entertainer and activist Josephine Baker is born in St. Louis, Missouri.

1919 Committed African American teacher and Director of the Woman's Bureau of the Department of Labor under President Nixon, Elizabeth Koontz is born in Salisbury, North Carolina.

1942 African American singer, songwriter, and producer, Curtis Mayfield is born in Chicago, Illinois. One of Mayfield's most recognizable songs is the theme song from the movie *Super Fly*.

1949 Wesley Brown is the first African American to graduate from Annapolis Naval Academy.

An arts festival celebrating Josephine Baker

US Senator Barack Obama campaigns at a rally in Rodney Square on February 3, 2008, in Wilmington, Delaware

JUNE 4

1913 Beneta Edwards is born in St. Paul, Minnesota. Edwards was an African American librarian, social worker, and community advocate.

1921 Tuskegee Airman and dentist, William Bethel Morgan was born in Homestead, Pennsylvania.

1922 Samuel Lee Gravely is born in Richmond, Virginia. He is the first African American to achieve the rank of vice admiral in the U. S. Navy.

1929 An enthusiast of Black history of Minneapolis-St. Paul and administrator, African American Walter Scott, Sr. is born in Greenville, Mississippi. Scott published his historical findings.

1972 African American militant activist Angela Davis is acquitted of conspiracy charges.

2008 Barack Obama is the first African American to win the Democratic Presidential nomination.

 ## JUNE 5

1885 The first edition of The *Western Appeal*, an African American newspaper in St. Paul, Minnesota is issued. The paper changes its name to *The Appeal* in 1888.

1920 One of the first African American professional football players, Marion Motley is born in Leesburg, Georgia.

1940 The American Negro Theater is formed to promote African American artists and community.

1945 John Wesley Carlos, 1968 Olympic bronze medalist who gave the "Black Power" salute on the podium with gold medalist Tommie Smith in, is born in Harlem, New York.

1950 Sweatt v. Painter is ruled on by the Supreme Court. This ruling declared that separate was not equal in this case, laying the groundwork for Brown v. Board of Education.

1950 The Supreme Court ruled similarly in the case of McLaurin v. Oklahoma Board of Education, as was ruled in Sweatt v. Painter.

JAN
FEB
MAR
APR
MAY
JUN
JUL
AUG
SEP
OCT
NOV
DEC

JUNE 6

1799 Black Russian poet and writer Alexander Pushkin is born in Moscow, Russia.

1885 Advocate of the Harlem Renaissance arts and successful businesswoman, A'Lelia Walker is born in Vicksburg, Mississippi.

1939 African American Marian Wright Edelman founder of the Children's Defense Fund is born in Bennettsville, South Carolina.

1958 The Detroit Tigers baseball team becomes integrated when African American Ozzie Virgil is acquired from the San Francisco Giants.

2004 Phylicia Rashad is the first African American to receive a Tony Award for a dramatic lead role on Broadway.

 # JUNE 7

1880 Chester Arthur Franklin, African American businessman, and publisher of the *Kansas City Call* is born in Denison, Texas.

1917 Gwendolyn Brooks, the first African American to receive a Pulitzer Prize for poetry, is born in Topeka, Kansas.

1927 African American sculptor and painter, Lilian Thomas Burwell, is born in Washington, D. C.

1943 Social activist, poet, and educator, Nikki Giovanni is born in Knoxville, Tennessee. Her children's book *Rosa* honors the work of Rosa Parks in the fight for civil rights.

1953 The Supreme Court rules in favor of Mary Church Terrell in her suit to end segregation in public restaurants and hotels in Washington, D.C.

1958 Mega music superstar Prince (birth name Prince Rogers Nelson) is born in Minneapolis, Minnesota. Prince received numerous accolades and awards for his music.

 ## JUNE 8

1868 The first African American to graduate from MIT and the first to receive a degree in architecture, Robert Taylor is born in Wilmington, North Carolina. He worked with Booker T. Washington to design and build the campus of Tuskegee Institute.

1892 Homer Plessy boards a whites only railroad car and refuses to move to the blacks only car. Setting in motion the landmark case of Plessy v. Ferguson.

1862 African American sharecropper and union organizer,

JAN
FEB
MAR
APR
MAY
JUN
JUL
AUG
SEP
OCT
NOV
DEC

Robert Hill is born in Dermott, Arkansas.

. . . .

1943 Olympic gold medalist in the 110-meter hurdles and U. S. Army National Guard Colonel, Willie Davenport is born in Troy, Alabama. Davenport was the first African American to participate in the Winter Olympics in the bobsled.

. . . .

1977 Paramount African American singer, rapper and producer Kanye West is born in Atlanta, Georgia.

. . . .

Kanye West and Jay Z at the world premiere of JAY-Z'S FADE TO BLACK on November 5, 2004, in New York

 ＪＵＮＥ 9

1845 African American education advocate, businessman and politician, James Napier is born in Nashville, Tennessee.

. . . .

1877 Meta Vaux Warrick is born in Philadelphia, Pennsylvania. Vaux Warrick was a prolific sculptor, who depicted the struggles of

African Americans in her work.

1911 The National Training School for Girls and Women in Washington, D. C. holds their first commencement. It was one of the first formal schools for African American women.

1934 African American R&B and soul singer, Jackie Wilson is born in Detroit, Michigan. Wilson's biggest hit was "Your Love Keeps Lifting Me."

1964 Professional basketball player and musician Wayman Tisdale is born in Tulsa, Oklahoma.

1980 The "Presidential Medal of Freedom" is awarded to Clarence Mitchell, Jr., a civil rights activist, by President Jimmy Carter.

 ## JUNE 10

1794 The Bethel African Methodist Church is founded in Philadelphia by Richard Allen.

1854 The first African American Catholic Bishop, James Augustine Healey, is ordained in Notre-Dame Cathedral in Paris, France.

1951 World renowned African American Agri-scientist and college and university administrator, Robert Jones is born in Dawson, Georgia.

1898 The first African American actress to win an Academy Award,

Hattie McDaniel, is born in Wichita, Kansas.

1902 African American Granville T. Woods receives the patent for the automatic air brake.

2007 Lewis Hamilton is the first Black to win a Formula One racing event at the Canadian Grand Prix.

 # JUNE 11

1854 Booker T. Washington's second wife and prime supporter of the creation of the Tuskegee Institute, Olivia Davidson, is born in Virginia.

1883 Founder of the Palmer Institute, a vocational school for African Americans, and civil rights advocate, Charlotte Hawkins (Brown) is born in Henderson, North Carolina.

1920 From Port of Spain, Trinidad, Black singer, actress and social activist, Hazel Scott is born.

1963 President John F. Kennedy gives his "Civil Rights" speech, advocating for the Civil Rights Act.

1963 The University of Alabama admits its first two African American students, Vivian Malone, and James Hood. The two are escorted by the U. S. Deputy Attorney General, Nicholas Katzenbach.

JUNE 12

1808 The Abyssinian Baptist Church in New York City is organized.

1904 Negro League pitcher Willie Foster is born in Calvert, Texas.

1912 African American actress and singer from the 1920s and 1930s, is born in Lancaster, South Carolina.

1930 African American woman Episcopal Bishop and civil rights activist, Barbara Harris is born in Philadelphia, Pennsylvania.

1963 Leading civil rights activist Medgar Evers is assassinated in Jackson, Mississippi.

1967 The Supreme Court announces its ruling on Loving v. Virginia. The Court ruled that the state could not restrict racially mixed marriages.

1969 The Black Academy of Arts and Letters is granted a charter by the state of New York.

JUNE 13

1868 Oscar J. Dunn is inaugurated as the first African American Lt. Governor of Louisiana, the first for any U.S. state.

JAN
FEB
MAR
APR
MAY
JUN
JUL
AUG
SEP
OCT
NOV
DEC

JAN
FEB
MAR
APR
MAY
JUN
JUL
AUG
SEP
OCT
NOV
DEC

1894 Provident Hospital in Baltimore, Maryland opens for the care of and benefit of the African American community of Baltimore.

1905 World-renowned trumpeter, Doc Cheatham is born in Nashville, Tennessee.

1937 African American lawyer, civil rights activist, and politician, Eleanor Holmes (Norton) is born in Washington, D. C.

1967 President Lyndon B. Johnson nominates Thurgood Marshall as the first African American to sit on the Supreme Court.

1991 Bernadette Locke is appointed assistant basketball coach at Division 1 University of Kentucky. She is the first African American woman to coach Division 1 Basketball.

 # JUNE 14

1811 Author and abolitionist Harriet Beecher Stowe is born in Cincinnati, Ohio. Stowe is the author of *Uncle Tom's Cabin*.

1854 Former slave accomplished cowboy and pullman porter, Nat Love is born in Davidson County, Tennessee.

1864 Congress enacts the Enrollment Act giving African American soldiers equal pay.

1891 African American John Standard is granted a patent for a refrigeration device.

....

1926 The first African American Major League pitcher to start a World Series game, Don Newcombe is born in Madison, New Jersey.

....

1939 Ethel Waters becomes the first African American woman to host a TV show.

....

Ethel Waters featured on a US postage stamp, circa 1994

 JUNE 15

1877 Henry O. Flipper becomes the first African American to graduate from West Point Academy, and the first African American commissioned officer in the regular Army.

....

1879 Abolitionist and social leader Josiah Henson is born in Maryland. Henson created a settlement where refugee slaves were taught to support themselves.

....

JAN FEB MAR APR MAY JUN JUL AUG SEP OCT NOV DEC

JAN
FEB
MAR
APR
MAY
JUN
JUL
AUG
SEP
OCT
NOV
DEC

1921 Poet innovator, educator and writer, African American James Emanuel is born in Nebraska.

1923 African American composer and piano great Erroll Garner is born in Pittsburgh, Pennsylvania.

1927 The daughter of two professional African American pianists, Natalie Hinderas is born in Oberlin, Ohio. Hinderas becomes a world-famous pianist, playing with many world-class symphonies.

1953 The African Americans of Baton Rouge, Louisiana begin the nation's first bus boycott. The successful boycott leads to a first come first served policy.

  JUNE 16

1896 Boston civic leader and educator African American Melnea Cass is born in Richmond, Virginia.

1898 Harlem Renaissance poet, writer, and teacher, Marita Bonner (Occomy) is born in Boston, Massachusetts.

1917 College administrator, AME Bishop, and educator, Rembert Stokes was born. Stokes instituted the practice of the Cooperative Education Program, which helps secure students with jobs in their field of study.

1920 White author John Griffin is born In Dallas, Texas. Griffin is best known for writing his experiences the book *Black Like Me*, in which he chemically colors his skin to appear black, allowing him to travel through the South as a Black man.

1927 Owner of Johnson Products, a cosmetics company, which was the first Black-owned business on the American Stock Exchange, George Johnson, Sr. is born in Richton, Mississippi.

1971 Best-selling rap artist and Tupac Shakur is born in the Bronx, New York.

 # JUNE 17

1775 Peter Salem and Salem Poor, freed slaves, received commendation for their service to the Americans in the Battle of Bunker Hill.

1861 Nettie Langston (Napier), African American social activist and organizer, is born in Oberlin, Ohio.

1930 Rosemary Brown is born in Jamaica. Brown immigrated to Canada and became a social activist and politician.

1849 Voting rights advocate, and politician, African American Thomas E. Miller is born.

1980 African American tennis

phenom, Venus Williams is born in Lynnwood, California.

1994 O. J. Simpson leads Los Angeles police on a low-speed chase through the freeways of Southern California. Simpson was wanted for questioning in the murder of his ex-wife, Nicole Brown Simpson.

Grand Slam champions Serena and Venus Williams during their first round doubles match at the US Open, 2013

JUNE 18

1793 Freed slave, abolitionist, plantation and slave owner, Anna Kingsley is born in Jai, Senegal.

1873 Tom Turpin, influential African American ragtime composer is born in Savannah, Georgia.

1939 Highly regarded African American math teacher, Genevieve Knight is born in Brunswick, Georgia.

1942 U. S. Navy commissions the first African American Naval Officer, Bernard Robinson.

1942 The second native African President of South Africa, Thabo Mbeki is born.

1991 Wellington Web is elected the first African American Mayor of Denver, Colorado.

JUNE 19

1865 The Emancipation Proclamation is read in Galveston, Texas, prompting a celebration by former slaves. The annual tradition continued and came to be known as Juneteenth. Juneteenth became a national holiday when President Joe Biden signed the bill into law on June 17, 2021.

1883 African American socialite and school photographer, Addison Scurlock is born in Fayetteville, North Carolina.

1912 Two hundred forty-five students are the first enroll in Tennessee A&I State Normal School for Negroes, later to become Tennessee State University (TSU). TSU is an HBCU.

1948 African American TV actress, Phylicia Rashad is born in Houston, Texas. Rashad is most noted for her role as Claire Huxtable in the Cosby Show.

1964 The Civil Rights Act of 1964 is passed by the U. S. Congress, proclaiming that segregation and

JAN
FEB
MAR
APR
MAY
JUN
JUL
AUG
SEP
OCT
NOV
DEC

discrimination based on race, color, national origin, or gender are illegal.

1968 The Poor People's March to bring attention to the plight of the poor and underserved populations in the U. S.

 # JUNE 20

1863 West Virginia becomes a state. After Virginia votes to secede from the United States to become part of the Confederate States of America the citizens of western Virginia vote to secede from Virgina, creating the new Unionist State of West Virginia.

1894 Food preservation scientist, and inventor Dr. Lloyd Hall is born in Elgin, Illinois.

1897 Influential African American educator and librarian Charlemae Hill (Rollins) is born in Yazoo, Mississippi. Rollins advocated for the realistic portrayal of African Americans in children's literature.

1920 Tuskegee Airman and administrator, Joseph Gomer is born in Iowa Falls, Iowa.

1928 Influential and pioneering African American saxophonist Eric Dolphy is born in Los Angeles, California.

1943 Detroit Race Riots take place resulting in 400 injuries and the deaths of 25 African Americans and 9 white individuals.

1960 Harry Belafonte becomes the first African American to win an Emmy.

📑 JUNE 21

1832 Former slave, congressman, and barber, Joseph Rainey is born in Georgetown, South Carolina.

1859 Internationally acclaimed African American artist Henry O. Tanner is born in Pittsburgh, Pennsylvania.

1879 African American lyricist of popular songs and singer, Henry Creamer is born in Richmond, Virginia.

1927 African American lawyer, judge, Mayor of Cleveland, TV news reporter, and ambassador, Carl Stokes is born in Cleveland, Ohio.

1936 African American singer and minister, O. C. Smith is born in Mansfield, Louisiana.

1964 Suspected members of the Ku Klux Clan murder 3 civil rights workers, Andrew Goodman, James Chaney, and Michael Schwerner.

1971 The (NOMA) is formed in Detroit, Michigan. NOMA organized to provide encouragement and opportunities for people of color within the field of architecture.

JAN
FEB
MAR
APR
MAY
JUN
JUL
AUG
SEP
OCT
NOV
DEC

JUNE 22

1865 African American blues and popular singer Eva Gibbons (Taylor) was born in St. Louis, Missouri.

2010 The first African American choreographer at the Metropolitan Opera in New York, anthropologist, and dancer, Katherine Dunham is born is Chicago, Illinois.

1937 Joe Louis becomes the heavyweight boxing champion of the world by defeating James J. Braddock.

1941 Twenty-time Emmy Award winner for journalism, African American CBS News correspondent Ed Bradley is born in Philadelphia, Pennsylvania.

1947 Award-winning science fiction writer, African American Octavia Butler is born in Pasadena, California.

1983 The Louisiana legislature repeals the last racial classification law in the United States.

JUNE 23

1913 Versatile African American singer Helen Humes is born in Louisville, Kentucky.

1928 African American artist, TV announcer, and civil rights activist, William Pleasant, Jr. is born in Savannah, Georgia.

1938 Educator and social activist, African American Charles McDew is born in Massillon, Ohio.

1940 African American Track star and three-time Olympic gold medalist Wilma Rudolph is born in Bethlehem, Tennessee.

1948 Supreme Court Judge, Clarence Thomas is born in Pinpoint, Georgia.

Clarence Thomas, Supreme Court justice nominee, testifies before the US Senate Judiciary Committee on September 12, 1991

 **JUNE 24**

1310(15) Philippa of Hainault is born in Northern France. (The year of her birth is not exactly known.) She becomes the first Black queen of England when she marries King Edward III.

1813 White abolitionist, social activist and clergyman, Henry Ward Beecher

is born in Litchfield, Connecticut.

1840 Former slave, educational activist, educator and politician, James Turner is born in St. Louis, Missouri. Turner was the first African American to serve in the U. S. diplomatic corps.

1911 World-renowned African Canadian singer, Portia White is born in Truro, Nova Scotia.

1914 African American caterer, civic leader, and businessman, Oscar Howard is born in Rochelle, Georgia.

1936 Mary McLeod Bethune is appointed Director of Negro Affairs of the National Youth Administration by President Franklin D. Roosevelt.

 # JUNE 25

1843 African American businessman and civic leader, Richard Burton Fitzgerald was born a free person of color in New Castle County, Delaware.

1850 Former slave, South Carolina state congressman, and clergyman, William Harrison Heard is born in Elbert County, Georgia.

1928 Professional football player for the Los Angeles Rams, and Pittsburgh Steelers, Paul Younger was born in Grambling, Louisiana. Younger became the first African American NFL assistant general manager.

1933 James Meredith is born in Kosciusko, Mississippi. Meredith is the first African American to attend the University of Mississippi.

1941 An executive order forbidding discrimination in the defense industries is issued by Pres. Franklin D. Roosevelt, creating the Fair Employment Practices Commission.

1975 Mozambique wins independence from Portugal through a resistance coup, The Carnation Revolution.

 # JUNE 26

1937 Born in Louisville, Kentucky, Robert Louis Thompson is a Black artist and painter known for his figurative expressionist paintings.

1956 Dr. Bernard A. Harris, the first African American astronaut to perform a spacewalk is born in Temple Texas.

1964 Florida governor dispatches state troopers to St. Augustine as race riots surge.

1974 Outstanding African American short stop, hitter, and part owner and CEO of the Florida Marlins, Derek Jeter is born in Pequannock Township, New Jersey. Jeter spent his entire 20-year

JAN
FEB
MAR
APR
MAY
JUN
JUL
AUG
SEP
OCT
NOV
DEC

JAN
FEB
MAR
APR
MAY
JUN
JUL
AUG
SEP
OCT
NOV
DEC

baseball career with the New York Yankees.

1978 Supreme Court rules racial quotas are unconstitutional in Regents of the University of California v. Bakke.

2005 The NAACP elects retired telecommunications executive Bruce Gordon as its president.

New York Yankees shortstop Derek Jeter on August 14, 2012, at Yankee Stadium

JUNE 27

1872 Internationally recognized prolific poet and writer, African American Paul Lawrence Dunbar is born in Dayton Ohio.

1894 The first African American woman to be elected to state office, Crystal Fauset is born in Princess Anne, Maryland.

1919 Civil rights leader, executive and publisher, M. Carl Holman is born in Minter City, Mississippi.

1922 Accomplished African American classical pianist George T. Walker is born in Washington, D. C.

1925 Founder of 31 schools for the deaf across Africa, deaf African American

Andrew Foster is born in Ensley, Alabama.

1933 African American research and development electrical engineer, Caldwell McCoy is born in Hartford, Connecticut.

 JUNE 28

1866 With authorization by the U. S. Congress, the two Black calvary units and four Black infantry units were created. The two calvary units were known as the Buffalo Soldiers.

1890 Track athlete, coach and judge, African American Howard Drew is born in Lexington, Kentucky. Drew was the first elected Black judge in the state of Connecticut.

1910 African American actress on Broadway, TV and movies, Ruth Attaway is born in Greenville, Mississippi.

1951 The Television program "Amos 'n' Andy" was first aired. It was pulled from syndication in 1966 for its negative portrayals of African Americans.

1971 African American Muhammad Ali's conviction for draft evasion is overturned by the

Supreme Court. Ali refused to register for the draft as a conscientious objector.

2012 The Montford Point Marines, established in 1942 and the first group of African Americans to enter the Marine Corps, are awarded the Congressional Gold Medal.

JUNE 29

1863 William Henry Hunt, one of the first African American members of the United States diplomatic core, is born.

1943 Versatile singer of the 1960s, Eva Boyd, known as Little Eva, is born in Belhaven, North Carolina. The song "The Loco-Motion" was written for her by Carole King and Gerry Goffin.

1867 African American singer, educator, and advocate for the "Negro Spiritual," Emma Smith (Hackley) is born in Murfreesboro, Tennessee.

1886 Photographic chronicler of the Harlem Renaissance, African American James Van Der Zee is born in Lenox, Massachusetts.

1951 Mabel K. Staupers receives Spingarn for her leadership in the field of nursing.

1941 Stokely Carmichael, radical social activist is born in Port of Spain, Trinidad, West Indies.

1969 This is the first day of the Harlem Cultural Festival. The festival held a 6-concert series to promote African American culture and accomplishments.

 ## JUNE 30

1917 Lena Horne, national award-winning singer and first African American to sign a contract with a major movie studio, is born in Brooklyn, New York.

1930 Economist, writer, and social advocate, Thomas Sewell is born in Gastonia, North Carolina.

1934 African American stage, screen and TV actor, Ted Ross is born in Zanesville, Ohio. Ross won a Tony Award for The Cowardly Lion in *The Wiz*.

1956 Winner of multiple Emmy Awards television and movie director, and producer, African American Paris Barclay is born in Chicago Heights, Illinois.

1971 Morris Dees and Joe Levin establish the Southern Poverty Law Center in Montgomery, Alabama as a resource for civil rights advocacy.

1974 Alberta W. King, mother of Martin Luther King, Jr., is shot and killed while playing the organ in church.

JAN
FEB
MAR
APR
MAY
JUN
JUL
AUG
SEP
OCT
NOV
DEC

JULY 1

1877 Benjamin O Davis is born in Washington D.C. Mr. Davis is noted as the first African American general in the modern era of the United States military.

1911 Journalist and news publisher, Lucile Bluford, was born in Salisbury, N. Carolina. As editor of *The Kansas City* Call Ms. Bluford led the civil rights movement and made the paper of national importance to the African American community.

1988 Atlanta University and Clark College are merged to form Clark Atlanta University. It is recognized as one of more than 100 historical Black colleges and universities.

2002 Black Farmers stage a prayer/sit-in protest and bring attention to the plight of African American Farmers being denied or being delayed operation loans they were legally entitled.

JULY 2

1777 The independent country of Vermont abolishes slavery. It is the first colonial country to prohibit the practice of slavery.

1822 Abolitionist, Demark Vesey, is hanged for conspiring to raise the largest slave revolt in American history.

1925, Medgar Evers civil rights activist is born in Decatur, Mississippi. His assassination was the first of a civil rights martyr which led to the passage of the civil rights act of 1964.

1828 The Oblate Sisters of Providence is established being the first African American order of nuns in the Catholic church. The community is composed of free Black women to educate African American children.

1908 Thurgood Marshall lawyer and Supreme court justice is born. Mr. Marshall was a significant figure in the victory of the case of Brown V. Board of Education of Topeka (1954), a case regarding racial segregation in public schools.

1964 Civil Rights Act is enacted. President Lyndon B Johnson signed the bill that specifically prohibited discrimination in voting, education, and public facilities.

1968 The African American Museum and Library at Oakland is established. It is the first library in Oakland to have a collection dedicated to the collection, preservation, and access to the history of African Americans in the West.

JAN FEB MAR APR MAY JUN JUL AUG SEP OCT NOV DEC

Bill Withers at the Ray Parker Jr. Hollywood Walk of Fame Star Ceremony on March 6, 2014

 # JULY 3

1855 Journalist, Black Feminist, and educator, Gertrude Mossell was born in Philadelphia, Pennsylvania. She wrote for the leading Black and White newspapers and magazines such as Woman's Era and the Ladies Home Journal.

1869 Joseph Douglass, violinist, and composer is born in Washington, D. C. The Black press applauded him as the most talented violinist of his race at the Chicago World's Fair.

1904 Dr. Charles Drew was born in Washington, D. C. The African American medical innovator is noted for improving the techniques allowing for greater quantities of blood to be stored.

1913 African American baseball player Lorenzo Piper Davis is born in Piper, Alabama. Mr. Davis is lauded as one of the most versatile players in baseball history.

He is recognized as being able to play any position expertly.

1950 The Hazel Scott Show premiered on network television. Ms. Scott became the first African American woman to have her own television show.

 ## JULY 4

1776 The American Declaration of Independence is adopted.

1844 Edmonia Lewis, sculptor was born in Abany, New York. Edmonia is noted as the first woman sculptor of African and Native American heritage. Her best-known work from 1867 is "Forever Free."

1883 African American Mary Peck Bond established Lemington Elder Care Services in Pittsburgh. It is one of the first homes dedicated to the care of aged and debilitated Black women. It is also the oldest continuously operated home of elder care in the United States.

1883 Soldier, athlete, and coach, Sammuel L. Ransom, is born in Chicago, Illinois. Ransom played baseball, football, and basketball in college and played with the St. Paul Colored Gophers in the Negro Leagues.

1938 African American Bill Withers, singer and songwriter is born in Slab Fork, West Virginia. Mr. Withers is known for

JAN FEB MAR APR MAY JUN JUL AUG SEP OCT NOV DEC

his classic R&B songs "Lean on Me," "Ain't No Sunshine," and "Just the Two of Us."

 ## JULY 5

1817 John Jones, politician is born a free man in North Carolina. The self-educated writer, businessperson, and abolitionist became one of the first black men to be elected to the senior office of Cook County Commissioner.

1852 Fredrick Douglass, abolitionist, gave the speech, "The Meaning of The Fourth of July for the Negro" at Corinthian Hall in Rochester, New York.

1947 The Cleveland Indians were the first baseball team to integrate the American Baseball League by signing Larry Doby.

1975 Tennis legend, Authur Ashe became the first African American to win the singles cup at Wimbledon.

 ## JULY 6

1863 Influential college professor and archaeologist John Westley Gilbert is born enslaved Hepzibah, Georgia.

1882 Booker T. Washington's personal

photographer, African American Arthur P. Bedou, is born in New Orleans, Louisiana.

1917 Jimmy Griffin, the first African American to rise to prominence in the St. Paul police force, is born.

1931 African American Della Reese, award-winning singer, and actress, is born in Detroit, Michigan.

She is best known for her role as Tess on the television show *Touched by an Angel*.

1937 Native South African writer and educator Bessie Head is born.

2006 The Wilberforce Institute for the Study of Slavery and Emancipation opens at the University of Hull in England.

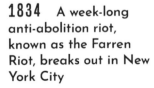 JULY 7

1834 A week-long anti-abolition riot, known as the Farren Riot, breaks out in New York City

1906 Baseball Hall of Fame pitcher Satchel Paige is born. He was the first African American pitcher in the American

League and in a World Series.

1950 The Population Registration Act 30 of South Africa, known as Apartheid, becomes law. This law required all citizens to register their race with the government.

JAN
FEB
MAR
APR
MAY
JUN
JUL
AUG
SEP
OCT
NOV
DEC

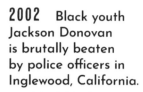

2002 Black youth Jackson Donovan is brutally beaten by police officers in Inglewood, California.

2022 Sandra Douglas Morgan becomes the president of the Las Vegas Raiders. She is the first African American woman to become president of an American national football team.

JULY 8

1923 Olympic gold-medalist in the 100 m sprint in 1948, and the 110 m hurdles in 1952, African American William Harrison Dillard is born in Cleveland, Ohio.

1826 White commander of the all Black 10th US Calvery, the famed Buffalo Soldiers, Benjamin Grierson is born in Pittsburgh, Pennsylvania. He was noted as a kind leader who puts his confidence and trust the abilities of his troops.

1855 Robert Boyd, doctor, teacher, and organizer of the society of colored Physicians and Surgeons is born in Giles County, Tennessee.

1876 The Hamburg Massare takes place during a riot between the Black militia and white neighbors of Hamburg, South Carolina. Six black men and one white man were killed in the riot.

1941 Hamilton Holmes, orthopedic surgeon and the first

African American to be accepted to Emery University School of Medicine, is born in Atlanta, Georgia.

....

1949 Hank Thompson, former player in Negro League, becomes the first African American to be signed to the New York Giants.

....

2003 President George W. Bush declares slavery as "one of the greatest crimes of history."

....

 ## JULY 9

1868 The 14th Amendment is approved, guaranteeing equal protection under the law for all people.

....

1893 African American Dr. Daniel Williams becomes the first to successfully perform open-heart surgery in the U.S.

....

1901 Actor, musical composer and arranger, Jester Hairston is born in Belew's Cree, North Carolina.

....

1972 Munto Dance Theater of Chicago is founded. Munto focuses on African and African American dance and folklore.

....

2002 Fifty-five African states join to create the African Union.

....

 ## JULY 10

JAN
FEB
MAR
APR
MAY
JUN
JUL
AUG
SEP
OCT
NOV
DEC

1875 Prominent educator and activist Mary McLeod Bethune is born in Maysville, South Carolina. She achieved national and international recognition for her commitment to education and the causes of the Black population.

1943 World-class African American tennis player Arthur Ashe is born in Richmond Virginia. He won many awards and accolades as a tennis player, Black advocate, and AIDS activist.

1945 Ron Glass, African American actor, is born in Evansville, Indiana. He is best known for his role as Ron Harris on the TV show *Barney Miller*.

1955 E. Fredric Morrow becomes President Dwight D. Eisenhower's Administrative Officer for Special Projects, becoming the first African American to hold an executive position in a presidential cabinet.

Ron Glass in Los Angeles, California, September 22, 2005

1963 A sit-in at the Dizzyland restaurant in Cambridge, Maryland leads to physical confrontations between police and protesters.

1973 The island nation of the Bahamas receives independence from Great Britain.

JULY 11

1767 President and abolitionist John Quincy Adams is born. He argued the Amistad Africans should be allowed to live as freemen before the Supreme Court and won.

1905 W.E.B. DuBois and William M. Trotter meet with 29 others to create the first organized African American protest group, the Niagara Movement.

1939 Clara Adams-Ender is born in Willow Springs, North Carolina. She goes on to become the Army's first African American Nurse Corps officer.

1945 Award-winning African American author and playwright Richard Wesley is born in Newark, New Jersey.

1951 The Cicero, a suburb of Chicago, is center of one of history's largest race riots in the United States. An estimated 4,000 whites attacked an apartment building where a single African American family was permitted to move.

JULY 12

1787 An agreement during the Constitutional Convention allowing slaves to be counted as 3/5ths of a person in calculating the number of congressmen and electoral votes from each state was approved. This is known as the Three-fifths Compromise.

1899 Civil Rights leader and union organizer Edgar D. Nixon is born in Lowndes County, Alabama.

1910 Frances Wills is born in Philadelphia, Pennsylvania. She along with Harriet Pickens became the first women African American Naval officers.

1949 African American Frederick M. Jones is granted a patent for his mobile refrigeration unit.

1958 Tony Willliams, Black actress most noted for her role on *The Young and the Restless*, is born in Kingston, Jamaica.

1967 The Race Riots of Newark, New Jersey begin and last four days. By the end of the riots 26 people had died and over 1,000 others were injured.

JULY 13

1817 World-renowned Black singer Elizabeth Taylor Greenfield is born in Natchez, Mississippi.

1853 Justice George H. Williams decides the case of Holmes v. Ford. Nathaniel Ford took his slaves Robin Holmes, his wife, and youngest three children to Oregon. Holmes sued for the release of his family on the grounds that slavery was illegal in Oregon. He and his family received their freedom.

1863 The Draft Riots of New York City begin "Four Days of Terror" due to white men being drafted into the Union Army, leaving the emancipated slaves to take the vacated jobs.

1868 Science teacher Marcellus Neal is born in Lebanon, Tennessee. He is the first African American to graduate from Indiana University.

1921 Samuel Proctor is born in Norfolk, Virginia. He was an African American educator and minister who worked tirelessly for the passage of the Civil Rights Act of 1964 and received 45 honorary degrees.

2013 George Zimmerman is found not guilty in the shooting death of Black youth Trayvon Martin. The same day the hashtag Black Lives Matter began a global social movement.

George Washington Carver National Monument in Missouri

 # ᒍᑌᒪᎩ 14

1885 Sarah Goode receives a patent for her invention of the cabinet bed. It was the precursor to the Murphy bed that was patented in 1900.

1893 Spencer William, Jr., a pioneer in African American films and TV, is born in Vidalia, Louisiana.

1905 The New York Public Library opens the Schomburg Center for Research in Black Culture in Harlem.

1932 Aide to Malcom X and Muslim minister African American Benjamin Karim, is born in Suffolk, Virginia.

1935 African American Pittsburgh Pirates pitcher Earl Francis is born in Slab Fork, West Virginia.

1953 The George Washington Carver National Monument is dedicated in Diamond, Missouri. Carver was an African American agricultural scientist innovator who promoted the use of peanuts and organic farming methods.

2010   In celebration of 50 years of independence from France's colonial rule Black African soldiers from 13 African nations march in France's Bastille Day Parade.

JULY 15

1867   The first Black woman bank president, Maggie L. Walker is born in Richmond, Virginia. She was also founder of Richmond's Saint Luke Penny Saving Bank.

1914   Marcus Mosiah Garvy organizes the Universal Negro Improvement Association and African communities League. These organizations are formed to globally promote people of African ancestry.

1903   The first post-Civil War building financed, owned, designed, and built by African Americans built in Washington, D. C. is dedicated. It is known as the True Reformer Building.

1938   Ernie Barnes, professional Black football player and world-renowned artist, is born in Durham, North Carolina.

1961   Award-winning African American actor, producer and director, Forest Whitaker is born in Longview, Texas. He is best known for the movie *The Butler* and the Television series *Godfather of Harlem*.

JAN
FEB
MAR
APR
MAY
JUN
JUL
AUG
SEP
OCT
NOV
DEC

1969 Beth A. Brown, first African American woman to earn her doctorate in astronomy from the Department of Astronomy at the University of Michigan and noted astrophysicist, is born in Roanoke, Virgina.

 ## JULY 16

1838 One of the first African American US Marshalls west of the Mississippi, Bass Reeves, is born in Crawford County, Arkansas. It is rumored that the legend of Bass Reeves inspired the character the Lone Ranger.

1854 African American Elizabeth Jennings is physically removed by the conductor with the aid of a police officer from a New York streetcar. Ms. Jennings sued the company and won judgement. This ruling forced the desegregation of transportation in New York.

1863 The American Civil War Battle of Honey Springs is fought in the Oklahoma Indian Territory.

1882 Violette Anderson, the first Black woman admitted to practice before the US Supreme Court, is born London, England.

1899 The first African American woman to hold the office of district attorney in the state of New York, Eunice Carter is born in Atlanta, Georgia.

 JAN
FEB
 MAR
APR
MAY
JUN
JUL
 AUG
SEP
OCT
NOV
DEC

1947 Alexis Herman is born in Mobile, Alabama. She is to become the first African American woman to hold the office of United States Secretary of Labor.

 ## JULY 17

1791 Ground is broken for the Bethel AME Church in Philadelphia, Pennsylvania. The church known as Mother Bethel Church was a stop on the underground railroad.

1888 Mariam E. Benjamin receives the patent for her "Gong and Signal Chair," which is the basis for attendant lights used on airplanes. Benjamin was only the second African American woman to receive a patent.

1935 African American actor Diahann Carroll is born in the Bronx, New York. Carroll is known for her work on Broadway and television.

1944 An explosion at the Naval Ammunition Depot in Port Chicago, California kills 377 and injures over 1000 sailors and civilians. Most victims are African American.

1967 Three days of race riots in Cairo, Illinois are sparked by the doubtful suicide of African American Army Pvt. Robert Hunt.

1977 Influential African Americans of the day in the art community establish the Black Academy of Arts and Letters.

JAN
FEB
MAR
APR
MAY
JUN
JUL
AUG
SEP
OCT
NOV
DEC

The purpose of the organization is to bring awareness of the cultural and social contributions of African Americans.

 ## JULY 18

1858 Educator and wife of Booker T. Washington, Fannie Smith Washington is born in Malden, West Virginia.

1863 Sergeant William H. Carney is the first African American soldier to receive the Congressional Medal of Honor for bravery in action during the U.S. Civil War.

1899 The U.S. Patent Office grants a patent for a folding bed to African American inventor Leonard C. Bailey.

1908 The philanthropical organization, the Frog Club, a group of African American members of the entertainment industry and other professionals.

1918 Antiapartheid leader and the first Black president of South Africa, Nelson Mandela is born in Umtata, South Africa. Madella received the Nobel Peace Prize in 1993.

1928 Eugene Hickman, an African American leader in pharmacology education, is born in Louisiana.

1946 Dianne McIntyre, world-renowned dancer, and choreographer, is born in Cleveland, Ohio.

  JULY 19

1866 Slavery is abolished within the Cherokee Nation by declaring all Cherokee as freedmen, as well as all African Americans living among the Cherokee Nation.

1867 A charter is granted to Saint Augustine's Normal School and Collegiate Institute to become one of the 100 HBCUs in the United States.

1881 African American laundresses in Atlanta, Georgia go on strike in effort to improve wages and working conditions.

1902 Cliff Jackson an innovative Black jazz stride pianist, is born in Culpeper, Virginia.

1909 This date marks the opening of the Piney Woods Country Life School in Rankin County, Mississippi. It is one of four historically Black boarding schools in the United States.

1946 Playwright Judy Juanita (born Judith Hart) is born in Berkeley, California. She was a professor of Black studies at San Francisco State University. The first such program in the United States.

JULY 20

JAN
FEB
MAR
APR
MAY
JUN
JUL
AUG
SEP
OCT
NOV
DEC

JAN
FEB
MAR
APR
MAY
JUN
JUL
AUG
SEP
OCT
NOV
DEC

1892 Joseph Ritter, archbishop of the St. Louis Archdiocese, is born in New Albany, Indiana. In 1947 Archbishop Ritter desegregated all of St. Louis' Catholic schools.

1909 African American Richard B. Spikes receives a patent for his Beer Tapper.

1934 Black poet and writer Henry Dumas is born. His works were published after being fatally shot by a New York Transit Authority Policeman.

1950 The U. S. Army's Black 24th Infantry Regiment gains the first American victory in the Korean War.

2002 The Alabama State Bar Association elects its first African American president, Fred Gray, Sr. He is the attorney who represented Rosa Parks in her bus segregation case.

 ## JULY 21

1802 White abolitionist David Hunter is born in Washington, D.C. He served as a colonel in the Union Army and openly advocated for emancipation.

1818 Abolitionist and educational advocate for Blacks, African American Charles Reason is born in New York.

1837 Hellen Appo is born in New York. She was an important member of the Black women's movement of her time.

1864 The first African American newspaper, *La Tribune de la Nouvelle Orle'ans*, in the United States releases its first edition in New Orleans, Louisiana.

....

1896 The National Association of colored Women's Clubs is established in Washington, D.C. Included in their objectives are the goals to promote and foster the education, welfare, and rights of women and children.

....

1959 African American Pumpsie Green plays for the Boston Red Sox. The Red Sox are the last major league baseball team to become integrated.

....

2002 The first edition of *The Liberator* magazine debuts. Its focus is to inform and promote cultural topics of importance and interest to Blacks.

....

📄 JULY 22

1510 Rumored son of an African house servant and Lorenzo II de' Medici, Alessandro de' Medici is born in Florence, Italy. Alessandro became the first ruler in western Europe of African descent.

....

1916 The American Tennis Association, the first African American sports organization is established to organize and promote tennis tournaments nationally and foster friendships through the sport of tennis.

....

JAN
FEB
MAR
APR
MAY
JUN
JUL
AUG
SEP
OCT
NOV
DEC

1922 The first Black woman to model in Paris for designers such as Christian Dior, Dorthea Church, was born in Texarkana, Texas.

1945 African American actor Danny Glover is born in San Francisco, California. He is most recognizable from the Lethal Weapon movies.

1964 British Parliament grants Gambia its national independence.

1967 The first American Black Power Conference is held in Newark, New Jersey. Their purpose was to discuss the most important and timely issues facing African Americans at that time.

1969 A race riot took place in York, Pennsylvania after the shooting death of African American Lillie Belle Allen. National Guard troops were called in to restrain the protesters.

 JULY 23

Corbin Bernsen and Danny Glover arrive at the grand opening of the Planet Hollywood night club in 1993.

1849 Marie Selika Williams, African American classical singer, is born in Natchez, Mississippi. She sang for such notable people as Pres. Rutherford Hayes and Queen Victoria.

1889 African American W. A. Martin receives a patent for the modern cylinder lock.

1891 Lewis Tompkins Wright is born in La Grange, Georgia. Wright was a prominent and respected African American surgeon and medical equality advocate.

1894 Accomplished African American artist and teacher, Hilda Rue Wilkinson Brown is born in Washington, DC.

1909 The first Pan-African conference is held in London, England.

1909 Black abstract expressionist painter Norman Lewis is born in Harlem, New York. His paintings brought wider acceptance to this style of painting.

1967 One of the largest race riots to date begins in Detroit, Michigan. At the end of the five-day uprising 43 people had died and 7231 people were arrested.

1892 Ethiopian dictator Halie Selassie is born in Harer, Ethiopia.

 JULY 24

JAN
FEB
MAR
APR
MAY
JUN
JUL
AUG
SEP
OCT
NOV
DEC

1802 Black French novelist Alexandre Dumas is born in Villers-Cotterets, France. Dumas is best known for several perennial classics including, *The Count of Monte Cristo*, *The Three Musketeers*, and *The Man in the Iron Mask*.

1892 African American chemist Alice Ball is born in Seattle, Washington. She was the first African American to receive her master's degree from the College of Hawaii.

1893 Charles Spurgeon Johnson, African American sociologist is born in Bristol, Virginia. He was the first Black president of Fisk University in Nashville, Tennessee.

1908 African American Cootie Williams, jazz trumpeter is born in Mobile, Alabama. Williams won acclaim for his trumpet muting techniques and brought his unique sound to the bands of Duke Ellington and Benny Goodman.

1914 Kenneth Clark, African American psychologist, is born in Harlem, New York. He is most noted for his work in the psychology of segregation.

1921 Award-winning African Anerican composer and jazz pianist Billy Taylor is born in Greenville, North Carolina. Taylor won distinction as an advocate for jazz music.

1934 African American William Davis is born in Lisbon, Louisiana. Davis played defensive end for the Green Bay Packers from 1960-1969.

JULY 25

JAN
FEB
MAR
APR
MAY
JUN
JUL
AUG
SEP
OCT
NOV
DEC

1806 Maria Weston Chapman, a white abolitionist, is born in Weymouth, Massachusetts. Maria Chapman was one of the founding members of the New England Anti-Slavery Society.

1912 Ann Moore Gregory, the first African American to enter the U. S. Amateur Golf Championships, is born in Aberdeen, Mississippi.

1941 Emmett Till is born in Chicago, Illinois. Emmett Till is immortalized as the African American teen who was kidnapped and murdered by two white men in Money, Mississippi in August 1955, which brought a national spotlight on the injustices occurring to African Americans, especially in the South.

1946 Two African American couples, Roger and Dorothy Malcom, and George and Mary Dorsey are murdered by a mob of white men in the Monroe Massacre, on Moore's Ford Bridge in Georgia.

1954 Declared one of the best running backs in National Football League history, African American Walter Payton, is born in Columbia, Mississippi. Payton played 13 seasons with the Chicago Bears.

2003 President George W. Bush assistance to aid West African allies by posting U.S. military off

the coast of Liberia, as a deterrent to the regional conflicts created by Liberian President Charles Taylor.

2003 National Football League commissioner Paul

Tagliabue fines the Detroit Lions for not interviewing a minority for the head coach position, as the NFL attempts to increase the number of minorities in leadership positions.

 JULY 26

1842 The Republic of Liberia gains independence from the United States. Liberia was a colony settled in Africa for free Africans in the United States

1894 African American stage and screen actress Mercedes Gilbert is born in Jacksonville, Florida.

1898 Edgar G. Brown, African American lobbyist and activist is born in Sandoval, Illinois.

One of his major successes was to see the prohibition of racial discrimination in federal civil service jobs.

1901 African American John Atkinson is born in Crawfordville, Georgia. Atkinson was the first State Park Superintendent in Georgia at the George Washington Carver State Park.

1911 The first Universal Races

Congress is convened at the University of London in efforts to improve race relations throughout the world.

1934 Black writer, journalist, educator, and politician, Austin Clarke, is born in Barbados. He is known for helping to establish Black studies departments at several universities in the United States.

1948 The Bob Howard Show premiers on CBS television as the first weekly nationally broadcast TV show featuring an African American host.

 ## JULY 27

1787 The South African Zulu monarch Shaka Zulu is born around this time. He was an influential leader and built a fierce military fighting force.

1815 An attack on the Negro Fort, Fort Gadsden, by U.S. armed forces in Florida began the Seminole Wars. At the time free and enslaved African Americans, Seminole and Choctaw Natives were living in the fort. The assault killed over 300 people taking refuge in the fort.

1856 Born in Canada, physician Nathan Mossell is born. Mossell was the first Black doctor to earn membership in the Philadelphia County Medical Society.

1884 P. B. Young, an African American newspaper publisher and editor, is born

JAN
FEB
MAR
APR
MAY
JUN
JUL
AUG
SEP
OCT
NOV
DEC

JAN
FEB
MAR
APR
MAY
JUN
JUL
AUG
SEP
OCT
NOV
DEC

Major William Lauderdale atop the Seminole War memorial statue

in Littleton, North Carolina. Young established the Norfolk Journal and Guide which became an important news outlet for African Americans in the South.

1897 African American William J. Powell is born in Henderson, Kentucky. Powell was a pioneer in the aviation industry, establishing the Bessie Coleman Aero Club and the first all-Black stunt air show in Los Angeles.

1919 This date marks the beginning of the week-long Chicago Race Riots. During that time 38 people were killed and over one thousand homes were destroyed.

1929 African American rhythm and Blues and doo-wop singer Harvey Fuqua is born in Louisville, Kentucky. Fuqua eventually became a producer of acts such as Marvin Gaye and Tammi Terrell, and David Ruffin.

 JULY 28

1855 The USS Constitution, a ship in the African Squadron, is commissioned by the US Navy. The African Squadron was a unit of the Navy tasked with the prevention of the transport of slaves from Africa to the United States.

1866 The Buffalo Soldier regiment, the 24th Infantry of the United States Cavalry is formed. Buffalo Soldiers were units of African American soldiers and white officers.

1915 After the unrest in Haiti following the murder of Hati dictator President Vilbrun Guillaume Sam, U.S. President Woodrow Wilson sends over 300 Marines to subdue the violence.

1917 The NAACP engaged in a silent protest rally in New York City to bring attention to the need for the U. S. Government to bring an end to lynchings and riots across the country in a time known as the "Red Summer of Hate." Nearly ten thousand African Americans participated in the protest.

1945 Evelyn Dilworth-Williams is born in Birmingham, Alabama. Williams had three poetry collections published that drew upon her life and the historical struggles of being African American.

2001 The Spady Cultural Heritage Museum, which is dedicated to the education and preservation of the history and culture of African Americans of the region, is established in Delray Beach, Florida.

JAN
FEB
MAR
APR
MAY
JUN
JUL
AUG
SEP
OCT
NOV
DEC

2014 Michelle Roberts become the first African American woman to head the National Basketball Players Association, or any professional sports union in the United States.

....

 ## JULY 29

1785 African French fencing champion, Jean Louis, is born in Haiti. Five-foot, 2-inch Louis' most famous match was dual to the death. The challenger was a six-foot-tall Spainard. Jean Louis won the match.

....

1805 White-French abolitionist Alexis de Tocqueville is born in Paris France. His most famous work is *Democracy in America* which is highly critical of the system of American slavery.

....

1870 The AME Church establishes Allen University in Cokesbury, South Carolina. Allen University is an HBCU.

....

1909 African American novelist Chester Himes is born. His most famous novels include *Cotton Comes to Harlem, The Real Cool Killers,* and *The Heat's On.*

....

1916 Pioneering African American jazz guitarist Charlie Christian is born in Dallas, Texas and was performing professionally by the age of 15.

....

1940 Jimmy McDaniel, Negro National Tennis Champion, is the first

African American to play in the American Tennis Association, in a challenge with Don Budge, the top American player at the time.

1978 Keeth Smart, internationally top ranked African American fencer, is born in Brooklyn, New York. Both he and his sister, Erinn Smart, won silver medals for fencing in the 2008 Olympics.

2003 The case against Officer Jeremy Morse for police brutality against Donovan Jackson is declared deadlocked and dismissed after the jury deliberated for more than three days.

  ## JULY 30

1863 President Abraham Lincoln issues General Order 252. This order is known as the "eye-for-an-eye" order. This order promised execution of one Confederate prisoner of war (POW) executed for each Black Union POW killed while in custody.

1930 White U. S. soldier and chauffeur Tony Vallelonga is born. He gained notoriety as a chauffeur hired to drive African American pianist Donald Shirley in the racially heated South in the 1960s.

1961 Distinguished award-winning African American actor, Laurence Fishburne is born in Augusta, Georgia. Fishburne is noted for his roles in *Boyz N the Hood*, the

Matrix movies, and *Akeelah and the Bee*.

1961 African American National Football League punter Reggie Roby is born in Waterloo, Iowa. Roby set a Pro Bowl punting record with 10 punts in a single game.

1967 Race riots in Milwaukee, Wisconsin last for four days. The riot began with a fight among teenagers in the area.

1970 Nelson Rockefeller, Governor of New York establishes the Medger Evers College in Brooklyn to meet the educational needs of the citizens in the borough of Brooklyn. The college is named in honor of Medgar Evers, a civil rights worker who was assassinated in Jackson, Mississippi.

 ## JULY 31

1911 The first African American Boy Scout troop is established in Elizabeth City, North Carolina.

1921 Outspoken African American civil rights activist and executive director of the National Urban League, Whitney Young is born in Lincoln Ridge, Kentucky.

1954 Internationally honored African American volleyball player Flo Hyman is born in Inglewood, California. Hyman helped the U. S. Olympic volleyball team bring home a silver medal in the 1986 Olympics.

1956 Deval Patrick, the first African American governor of Massachusetts, is born in Chicago, Illinois.

....

1968 The African American character Franklin and Charlie Brown meet in the comic strip Peanuts for the first time.

....

1972 An airplane bound for Miami, Florida is hijacked by members of the Black Liberation Army to Algiers. All 94 passengers and seven crew members were eventually released unharmed.

....

1981 African American Arnette

Hubbard becomes the first woman president of the National Bar Association.

....

Laurence Fishburne and Gina Torres at the premiere of *The Matrix Reloaded* in 2003.

AUGUST 1

1901 Whitesboro, New Jersey is founded. It was one of the many townships founded by African Americans after the Civil War.

1909 Mechanics and Farmers Bank is opened for business in Durham, North Carolina. This was one of the first African American savings and loans and the first lending institution in North Carolina to receive a certificate of authority from the Federal Housing Administration.

1917, The first issue of *The Messenger* is published. It is a literary and political magazine geared for African Americans that promoted the Harlem Renaissance.

1920 Henrietta Lacks was born. The African American mother and homemaker was the involuntary donor of cancer cells that created an immortal cell line for medical research.

1925 The National Bar Association is established. It is the country's largest and oldest association of African American judges and Lawyers.

 ## AUGUST 2

1825 Master Juba, a minstrel performer, is born. Mr. Juba is a dancer and is noted to be America's first officially recognized Black performer.

1924 African American author and critic, James Baldwin is born in New York City. Mr. Baldwin is recognized for his literary classic novels *Go Tell It on the Mountain, Nobody Knows My Name*, and *Giovanni's Room*.

1931 African American child prodigy, composer, and writer, Philippa Schuyler is born in New York, New York. Schuyler composed "The Rapsody of Youth" in honor of the inauguration of Haitian President Paul Magloire.

1966 Charles Drew University of Medicine and Science is founded. The University focuses on a curriculum that gives students skills to provide care for the poor and underserved populations.

2012 Gabrielle Douglas, 16, becomes the first African American to win the Olympic Artistic Gymnastics Women's Individual All-Around event.

Gabby Douglas at the Rio 2016 Summer Olympic Games

JAN
FEB
MAR
APR
MAY
JUN
JUL
AUG
SEP
OCT
NOV
DEC

AUGUST 3

1859 Charles Lewis Baker, inventor, was born. Mr. Baker is known for the invention of the friction heater. Baker established the Friction Heat and Boiler company in 1904.

1937 The Wings Over Jordan Choir is formed. The choir had radio program that featured the talents of Black singers. It was broadcast out of Cleveland, Ohio on the CBS network.

1952 A Black woman, Ruby McCollum, shot a white man, Dr. C Leroy Adams for years of physical abuse. Denied the opportunity to testify in her own trial, Ms. McCollum was found mentally incompetent and sentenced to a Florida State Hospital.

 # AUGUST 4

1810 Robert Purvis, the son of a white father and free woman of color is born in Charleston, South Carolina. Purvis was a steadfast abolitionist who used his position and influence to further the cause of abolition and women's rights.

1890 Effie Chamberlain and Belle Davis are the first African American entertainers to perform on an American stage in the production *Creoles*.

1901 One of the most recognizable entertainers of all time, African American Louis Armstrong is born in New Orleans, Louisiana. He is known for his unique singing voice and trumpet playing.

1936 African American John Woodruff wins a gold medal at the 1936 Olympics in the 800-meter race in Berlin, Germany.

1961 The first African American President of the United States, Barack Obama is born in Honolulu, Hawaii. Obama also served as an Ohio State Senator.

AUGUST 5

1763 The first African American boxer, William Richmond, is born in Cuckold's Town, Virginia. Richmond moved to England for a better life and took up boxing for self-defense.

1805 The African Meeting House in Boston is founded. The meeting house is also known as the First African Baptist Church and is the oldest Black church still standing in the United States.

1833 *An Appeal in Favor of that Class of Americans called Africans* is published. The book by white American author, Lydia Marie Child, favored the immediate

JAN FEB MAR APR MAY JUN JUL AUG SEP OCT NOV DEC

emancipation of Africans without compensation to slaveholders.

1880 Gertrude Rush, lawyer, and activist, is born in Navasota, Texas. Ms. Rush was admitted to the Iowa Bar in 1918 and was the state's first Black female lawyer.

1925 The Brotherhood of Sleeping Car Porters is founded. The labor organization was the first led by Blacks and first to receive a charter in the American Federation of Labor.

Statue of C. L. Dellums, one of the organizers and leaders of the Brotherhood of Sleeping Car Porters, in front of Jack London Square Station

 # AUGUST 6

1905 Librarian Miriam Matthews is born in Pensacola, Florida. Ms. Matthews was the first African American librarian in the Los Angeles Public Libraries.

1930 African American singer and actress known for her

social messages as well as her smooth singing voice, Abbey Lincoln is born in Calvin Center, Michigan.

1936 The Wake Robin Golf Club is established for African American women in Washington, D. C.

1948 Michael Peters, the African American choreographer for stage, screen, and TV, is born in Brooklyn, New York. He is best known for his work choreographing Michael Jackson's "Thriller," and "Beat It."

1962 Jamaica receives independence from Great Britain.

1965 The American Voting Rights Act is signed into law by President Lyndon B. Johnson. The law prevented practices that prevented or limited the voting rights of many African Americans in the South.

 # AUGUST 7

1894 Mark Matthews, the last of the Buffalo Soldiers, is born in Greenville, Alabama. Matthews died on September 6, 2005, being 111 years old.

1903 White anthropologist Louis Leakey is born in Kabete Mission, Kenya. Leakey organized and participated in many archaeological digs in Kenya and found many significant artifacts attributed to early humans.

JAN
FEB
MAR
APR
MAY
JUN
JUL
AUG
SEP
OCT
NOV
DEC

JAN
FEB
MAR
APR
MAY
JUN
JUL
AUG
SEP
OCT
NOV
DEC

1904 The first African American to win the Nobel Peace Prize, Ralph J. Bunche, is born in Detroit, Michigan.

1945 African American professional football player and Minnesota Supreme Court Judge, Alan Page is born in Canton, Ohio.

1946 Isaac Hathaway, an African American sculptor, is chosen to create the Booker T. Washington fifty-cent piece for the United States Mint.

1948 Alice Coachman becomes the first Black woman athlete to win an Olympic Gold Medal in any sport. She won the gold by jumping 5 feet 6 1/8 inches in the women's high jump.

1960 The Ivory Coast receives independence from France.

1989 African American congressman George Thomas Leland dies in a plane crash while traveling to a refugee camp in Fugnido, Ethiopia.

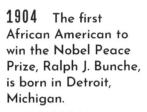

AUGUST 8

1796 The Boston African Society is founded as a mutual aid society to help members with social support and provide health and death benefits.

1861 The American Missionary Association founded the Freedmen's Aid Society for the purpose of providing teachers in the South for those who are emancipated.

1866 Mathew Henson, African American member of the first expedition to the North Pole, is born in Charles County, Maryland.

1921 Pediatrician Helen Nash, the first African American woman on the staffs of the St. Louis Children's Hospital and the Washington University School of Medicine, is born in Atlanta, Georgia.

1923 African American blues singer Jimmy Whitherspoon is born in Gurdon, Arkansas.

1950 Richard B. Spikes is awarded a patent for his Horizontally Swinging Barber's Chair.

1953 The first African American to be appointed as commander of the United States Central Command, and Secretary of Defense under President Joe Biden, Lloyd James Austin III is born in Mobile, Alabama.

 # AUGUST 9

1526 The first arrival of slaves in the American Colonies occurs on the coast of what is to become the state of South Carolina.

1884 Daisy Lampkin, an African American civil rights activist, and suffragist, is born in Washington, D.C.

1905 The first African American congressman to

JAN
FEB
MAR
APR
MAY
JUN
JUL
AUG

SEP

OCT
NOV

DEC

represent Pennsylvania, Rober Nix, Sr. is born in Orangeburg, South Carolina.

1948 White reporter Ray Sprigle's account as a Black man in the South is published in the Pittsburgh Post-Gazette.

1963 Global African American singing sensation Whitney Houston is born in Newark, New Jersey. Houston has the most awards of any female singer.

1967 African American Dion Saunders, the only athlete to play in both the Super Bowl of football and the World Series of Baseball, is born in Fort Myers, Florida.

1970 After 150 Black protesters marched on the Notting Hill police station in England, nine were arrested and tried for inciting a riot. The "Mangrove Nine" were found not guilty after a fifty-five day trial.

Whitney Houston at the 2007 Clive Davis Pre-Grammy party in Los Angeles

AUGUST 10

1858 Scholar, teacher, social and women's activist Anna Julia Haywood Cooper is born in Raleigh, North Carolina. Cooper was one of the first African American women to receive her PhD. In the U. S.

1880 The co-composer of the award-winning opera, *Ouanga*, African American Clarence White is born in Clarksville, Tennessee.

1905 The African American writer and editor Era Thompson is born in Des Moines, Iowa. Thompson worked as an editor for *Ebony* magazine for over 20 years.

1909 African American judge and congressman, George Crockett is born in Jacksonville, Florida. While on the Congressional Committee on Foreign Affairs, he strongly voiced his support of the anti-apartheid movement in South Africa.

1918 Arnett Cobb, African American jazz tenor saxophonist and Grammy winner, was born in Houston, Texas.

1929 The beginnings of the largest African American parade in the U. S., the first Bud Billiken parade is held in Chicago, Illinois.

1934 One of the first African American owned newspapers in Minnesota, the Minnesota Spokesman-Recorder, sells its first edition.

JAN
FEB
MAR
APR
MAY
JUN
JUL
AUG
SEP
OCT
NOV
DEC

1943 Black girl-group singer Ronnie Bennett Spector is born in Spanish Harlem neighborhood of New York. Spector was the lead singer in the group the Ronettes.

2023 Sixteen-year-old African American Shania Shakura Muhammad becomes the youngest full-time, credentialed, paid teacher in U. S. history.

 # AUGUST 11

1897 The Cleveland Home for Aged Colored People opens to eventually become the nation's oldest independent organization to support elderly African Americans.

1921 The author of the tremendously popular *Roots* and *Malcom X*, Alex Haley, is born in Ithaca, New York. The book *Roots* brought to light the realities of slavery to the American public and inspired many to research their own family genealogy.

1925 African American journalist, Ambassador to Finland, and director of the U. S. Information Agency, Carl Rowan is born in Ravenscroft, Tennessee.

1965 Riots in the south-central neighborhood of Los Angels known a Watts. The six-days of civilian unrest in the area resulted in 34 dead, more than 1000 injured, and $40 million in property damage.

1960 A former colony of France, the African

country of Chad is granted independence.

1965 The first African American woman to win Tony, Oscar, and Emmy awards, Viola Davis is born in ST. Matthews, South Carolina. Davis is known for her roles in *The Help, Doubt, and How to get Away with Murder*.

1967 The performing group the Watts Prophets is formed. Hip-hop music and culture is an out-growth of this music.

AUGUST 12

1825 Orindatus Simon Bolivar Wall, a freeman of color and the first Black captain in the Union Army, is born in Richmond County, North Carolina.

1838 The inventor of a paper-bag-making machine, and other inventions, William Purvis is born in Pennsylvania.

1862 Jewish American philanthropist Julius Rosenwald is born in Springfield, Illinois. His charity, the Rosenwald Fund, donated over $70 million to schools, colleges, and museums for both African Americans and Jewish Americans.

1866 Thomas Calloway, African American lawyer, is born in Cleveland, Tennessee. Calloway is known for his work on the exhibit featuring the advancements of African Americans at

JAN FEB MAR APR MAY JUN JUL AUG SEP OCT NOV DEC

the Paris Exposition in 1900.

1935   Alfred Bennett Spellman, African American writer and poet is born in Elizabeth City, North Carolina. In addition to his writings Spellman also worked for the National Endowment for the Arts to promote the Arts in Education program.

1937   Award-winning and nationally acclaimed youth author African American Walter Dean Myers is born in Martinsburg, West Virginia. He is best known for his books *Scorpions*, *Fallen Angels*, and *Monster*.

1987   Afro Swedish radio personality Amie Bramme Sey is born in Stockholm, Sweden.

AUGUST 13

1885   Lena O. Smith, the first African American women lawyer in Minnesota, is born in Lawerence, Kansas. Smith was an advocate for the rights of African Americans.

1892   The Baltimore Afro American Newspaper is established. The paper continues to be published in Baltimore, Maryland and Washington, D.C.

1904   The first African American music publishing company, the Attucks Music Publishing Company, is established in New York, New York.

1911   U. S. District Court Judge appointed by John F. Kennedy, James Parsons is born in Kansas City, Missouri.

1917 African American actress Claudia McNeil is born in Baltimore, Maryland. She is best known for her roles on Broadway in the productions *A Raisin in the Sun* and *The Crucible*.

1933 Joycelyn Elders, African American doctor, and former Surgeon General of the United States is born in Schaal, Arkansas.

1982 Shani Davis, the first African American to win an individual Gold Medal in speed skating, is born in Chicago, Illinois.

 # AUGUST 14

1858 The first African American to graduate from the University of Minnesota, Andrew Hilyer is born in Georgia.

1911 The first African American woman journalist on a national news network and civil rights activist, Ethel Pyne is born in Chicago, Illinois.

1914 Herman Branson, an African American physicist, is born in Pocahontas, Virginia. Branson's studies of the structure of proteins led to the discovery of the alpha helix, the forerunner to the discovery of the DNA double helix.

1935 The Federal Theatre Project is established, incorporating the

Negro Theatre Unit, to provide work for unemployed actors, writers, and theater workers.

1959   One of the most prominent basketball players of all time, African American Magic Johnson, Jr. is born in Lansing Michigan.

1966   Award-winning African American actress Halle Berry is born in 1966. She received an Oscar for *Monster's Ball* and a Golden Globe for the TV movie *Introducing Dorothy Dandridge*.

2000   Anthony Ervin becomes the first African American to make the Men's U. S. Swimming Team.

Halle Berry at the 89th Annual Academy Awards in 2017

 # AUGUST 15

1818   Bridget "Biddy" Mason, a midwife and nurse, is born in Mississippi. As a slave Biddy walked from Mississippi to the free state of California. With hard work and ability to save she became one of the first African American women landowners in California.

1887 Eatonville, Florida becomes the first incorporated Black town in the United States.

1925 One of the most outstanding jazz pianists of his day, Black Canadian, Oscar Peterson is born in Montreal, Quebec, Canada. Peterson has made more than 200 recordings and won eight Grammy Awards.

1938 Outspoken congresswoman and civil rights activist Maxine Waters is born in St. Louis, Missouri.

1938 Cornelius Coffey becomes the first registered African American pilot in the United States.

1960 The Republic of the Congo receives independence from France.

1969 One of the world's most eminent African American dance troops and academies, the Dance Theater of Harlem is established.

 # AUGUST 16

1838 The second wife of Fredrick Douglas, Helen Pitts, white American teacher, and suffragist is born in Honeoye, New York.

1870 The U. S. Army commissions 13 Black Seminoles to form the

Black Seminole Indian Scouts to patrol the western frontier.

1927 African American U. S. Army soldier, William Thompson, is born in Brooklyn, New York. He was honored with the Medal of Honor for his dedication and bravery in battle.

1929 The first African American to sign with the Pittsburgh Pirates, Curt Roberts, is born in Pineland, Texas.

1931 A writer and social activist, Marion Patrick Jones, is born in Port of Spain, Trinidad and Tobago.

1939 The National Negro Airmen Association of America, an association for African American pilots, is formed in Chicago, Illinois.

1947 The first African American woman Senator, Carol Moseley Braun, is born in Chicago, Illinois.

2001 African American Stephanie Ready is becomes the first woman professional men's sports coach with the National Basketball Association's development team the Greenville Groove.

AUGUST 17

1894 Texas College holds its first classes in Tyler, Texas. It is one of the over one hundred HBCUs.

1918 African American jazz saxophonist, Ike Quebec is born in Newark, New Jersey.

1918 The first edition of the Negro World Newspaper is produced in New York City.

1932 Duke Pearson Jr., African American jazz pianist and composer, is born in Atlanta, Georgia.

1960 Gabon receives independence from France.

1961 Scottish African environmental activist, Aaron Mair, is born in Valhalla, New York.

AUGUST 18

1921 Howard Jones Jr., African American engineer and inventor is born in Richmond, Virginia. His most notable accomplishments include his research on the use of microwaves and the development of specialized air and space antenna.

1934 Baseball great Afro Puerto Rican, Roberto Clemente is born in Carolina, Puerto Rico. Clemente played 18 seasons with the Pittsburgh Pirates and won 12 Golden Glove awards.

1935 African American actress Gail Fisher is born in Orange, New Jersey. Fisher Is most recognizable from her role on the long running TV show *Manix*. She won an Emmy award for her

JAN
FEB
MAR
APR
MAY
JUN
JUL
AUG
SEP
OCT
NOV
DEC

work on the series *Room 222*.

. . . .

1935 African American portrait artist, Simmie Knox is born in Aliceville, Alabama. Knox is noted for his official portraits of President Bill Clinton and First Lady Hillary Clinton.

. . . .

1963 African American James

Meredith becomes the first Black student to graduate from the University of Mississippi.

. . . .

1964 The country of South Africa is banned from the Olympic games due to the apartheid laws and practices. The ban was lifted in 1992 when the oppressive apartheid policies were lifted.

. . . .

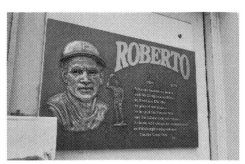

Roberto Clemente Bridge plaque at Sixth Street Bridge in Pittsburgh, Pennsylvania

 ## AUGUST 19

1826 Former slave Mansfield Tyler, Baptist preacher and U. S. Congressman

representing Alabama, is born near Augusta, Georgia.

. . . .

1906 Pioneering African American guitarist, Eddie Durham is born in San Marcos, Texas. Durham invented an amplified electric guitar.

1924 Retired African American U. S. Army Air Force officer and Tuskegee Airman, Harold Brown is born in Minneapolis, Minnesota. He was captured as a Prisoner of War in Germany when his plane was shot down. Brown was released at the end of the war.

1929 African American stage and TV actor, William Marshall is born in Gary, Indiana. Marshall's most well-known roles include the horror film *Blacula*, King of Cartoons on *Pee-Wee's Playhouse*," and his one-man show *Enter Fredrick Douglas*.

1977 William Hurd, former CIA agent, author, and the first Republican voted African American to the House of Representatives, is born in Leon Valley, Texas.

1989 Bishop Desmond Tutu of South Africa breaks the law by leading hundreds of Black Africans on a "whites only" beach in Cape Town.

 # AUGUST 20

1865 Wilberforce University is established in Greene County, Ohio. Wilberforce is the oldest private historically black university and was

previously a stop on the underground railroad.

1876 John Henry "Dick" Turpin, master diver and Naval officer, is born in Long Branch, New Jersey. Turpin was among the first African Americans to receive the rank of chief petty officer in the Navy.

1899 Roger Young, the first African American woman to earn her PhD. In zoology, is born in Clifton forge, Virginia.

1910 The African American settlement of Deerfield, Colorado is established.

1942 African American Issac Hayes,

singer and composer, is born in Covington, Tennessee. Heyes is most notably known for the soundtrack for the movie *Shaft*, for which he won an Oscar.

1941 William Gray III, a congressman from Pennsylvania, is born in Baton Rouge, Louisiana. He was the first African American to hold the congressional post of Majority Whip.

1962 Jonathan Daniels and Father Richard Morrisroe, white Civil Rights workers, were shot in Hayneville, Alabama. Daniels died from his wounds and Morrisroe was seriously injured.

 ## AUGUST 21

1791 Toussaint L'Ouverture leads a successful slave revolt in Haiti. The revolt is the beginning of an independent Haiti.

1831 Nat Turner's Slave Rebellion, also known as the Southhamption Insurrection, takes place in Southhampton County, Virginia. Turner leads a slave revolt supported by 60 other slaves from neighboring plantations, resulting in many deaths and more restrictive laws concerning Blacks.

1836 The decision of Commonwealth v. Aves declares any slave brought to the state for any length of time is entitled to freedom.

1860 White lawyer, judge, and abolitionist, Charles E. Vanderburgh rules to free Eliza Winston when she accompanies her Southern owners to the free state Minnesota.

1904 Among the most preeminent big band leaders Count Basie is born in Red Bank, New Jersey. Basie was the first African American man to receive a Grammy Award and led his band for over 50 years.

1928 African American jazz trumpeter Art Farmer is born in Council Bluffs, Iowa.

1936 One of the top-scoring basketball players of all time, African American Wilt Chamberlain is born in Philadelphia, Pennsylvania. He averaged over 30 points per game in his fifteen-year career.

1949 African American actress Loretta Devine is born in Houston, Texas. She is best known for the movie *Waiting to Exhale*.

JAN
FEB
MAR
APR
MAY
JUN
JUL
AUG
SEP
OCT
NOV
DEC

AUGUST 22

1792   The case of Brom and Brett v. Ashley is concluded by ordering John Ashley to release Elizabeth Freemen and another African American man. The case was brought to court on the grounds that the new Massachusetts State Constitution declared all people free.

1880   George Herriman, African American cartoonist, is born in New Orleans, Louisiana. Herriman was the creator of the comic strip *Krazy Kat*.

1885   African American union organizer and civil rights advocate Johns Artemus is born in Edgefield, South Carolina. He helped to create the United Brotherhood of Carpenters Union.

1898   One of the first African American owned insurance companies, North Carolina Mutual Life Insurance Company, is established in Durham, North Carolina.

1910   The Howard Theater in Washington, D.C. opens with acts and performances geared toward African American audiences.

1926   Biochemist and researcher, Dr. William Davis is born in Waycross, Georgia. Dr. Davis was the first African American to graduate with his Ph. D. from the University of Idaho. He made scores of medical and food discoveries and developments.

1934 Diana Sands, African American Actress, is born in the Bronx, New York. Her most prominent role was in both the stage and screen versions of *A Raisin in the Sun* as Beneatha Younger.

AUGUST 23

1791 The first International Day of Remembrance of the Slave Trade is held.

1853 The first African American doctor in North Carolina, James Shober, is born in Salem, North Carolina.

1892 African American Oscar Brown of Buffalo, New York is granted a patent for an improved horseshoe.

1900 The National Negro Business League is established by Booker T. Washington in New York City.

1954 Nigerian Philip Emeagwali, a computer scientist who was instrumental in creating the internet, was born in Onitsha, Nigeria.

1978 African American professional basketball player Kobe Bryant is born in Philadelphia, Pennsylvania. Bryant is considered one of the greatest basketball players of all time.

2004 The National Underground Railroad Freedom Center is dedicated in Cincinnati, Ohio.

AUGUST 24

1759 White English abolitionist, instrumental in the eradication of slavery in England, William Wilberforce, is born in Hull, England.

1867 One of America's over 100 Historically Black Colleges and Universities, Fayetteville State University in North Carolina is established.

1884 The first African American to be a registered civil engineer in the state of New York, George Biddle Kelley is born in Troy, New York.

1918 African American Augusta Dinkins, community advocate and proponent of cultural preservation, is born in Orlando, Florida.

1919 A member if the research team on the Manhattan Project, African American chemist Harlod Delaney is born in Providence, Rhode Island.

1972 African American film director and distributor Ava DuVernay is born in Long Beach, California. She was the first female African American to be nominated for an Academy Award for Best Picture for her film *Selma*.

1973 Dave Chappelle, African American comedian and actor, is born in Washington, D.C. He can be seen in the movie *Half-baked* and the TV series *Buddies*.

AUGUST 25

1854 Black Seminole scout for the U. S. Army, Isaac Payne, is born in Coahuila, Mexico. In 1875 Payne and two other scouts received the Congressional Medal of Honor after their heroic rescue of their commanding officer, John Bullis.

1886 The Lone Star State Medical, Dental, and Pharmaceutical Association is organized in Galveston, Texas. It is only the second professional medical association for African Americans in the United States.

1896 Black physician Alfred Waddell is born in Trinidad and Tobago. Waddell was also a social reformer by providing medical treatment to those who had no other access to help.

1904 Music composer, conductor and pianist, Undine Moore is born in Jarratt, Virginia. Moore was co-founder of the Black Music Center at Virginia State.

1922 Prezell Robinson, African American educator and college administrator, is born in Batesburg, South Carolina. Robinson served as president at St. Augustine College in North Carolina for twenty-eight years, and on numerous other boards and committees.

1927 African American tennis great,

Althea Gibson, is born in Silver, South Carolina. She was the first African American woman to play in and win the U. S. Nationals Tennis Tournament.

1944 The U. S. military supply operation known as the "Red Ball Express" begins in France to supply Allied troops during World War II. Most drivers on the "Red Ball" were African American.

 # AUGUST 26

1821 African American world-renowned landscape artist Robert Duncanson is born in Seneca, New York. His art inspired and influenced painters for generations.

1867 Robert Moton, lawyer, and president of Tuskegee Institute is born in Amelia County, Virginia. Morton was also the president of the National Negro Business League from 1900-1920.

1900 African American master painter Hale Woodruff is born in Cairo, Illinois. Woodruff is known for his murals at the Trevor Arnett Library at Clark Atlanta University titled The Art of the Negro.

1918 NASA space scientist and mathematician, Kathrine Johnson is born in White Sulphur Springs, West Virginia. Johnson's ground-breaking work in space science and the integration of African Americans and women in science made her the focus of the book and film *Hidden Figures*.

....

1938 David Sibeko, a Black South African, was an outspoken proponent of the anti-apartheid movement

in South Africa, is born in Johannesburg, South Africa.

....

1956 The first African American students to integrate a public school in the South walked into Clinton High School in Clinton, Tennessee.

....

The cast of *Hidden Figures* at the 48th NAACP Image Awards on February 11, 2017

AUGUST 27

1879 The publisher of the Pittsburgh Courier, a Black newspaper, Robert Lee Vann is born in Ahoskie, North Carolina. He was editor of the Courier for 30 years.

....

1905 African American actor and union organizer, Frederick O'Neal is born in Brooksville, Mississippi. He was involved heavily in the Actors' Equity

JAN
FEB
MAR
APR
MAY
JUN
JUL
AUG
SEP
OCT
NOV
DEC

Association and Associated Actors and Artists of America unions.

1936 African American Roger Banks is born in Albuquerque, New Mexico. A former Peace Corps volunteer, Banks is known for his dedication to changing social and legal barriers to African Americans.

1937 Alice Coltrane, African American jazz pianist and harpist, was born in Detroit, Michigan. She turned to writing and performing "spiritual jazz" after the death of her husband, John Coltrane.

1965 U. S. Air Force and commercial pilot, LeRoy Homer was born in Long Island, New York. Homer a decorated African American Air Force veteran was the copilot of United Flight 93 on 9/11. When the crew and passengers learned of the other hijackings, it was decided to overthrow the hijackers, forcing the hijackers to abandon their target and crash the plane into a Pennsylvania field. The crash killed all on board.

Fredrick Douglass public bronze bust sculpture on the brick waterfront walkway at Fells Point

AUGUST 28

1863 The 14th U.S. Colored Heavy Artillery Regiment is organized in Providence, Rhode Island for service during the Civil War.

1895 The Fredrick Douglas Memorial Hospital is established in Philadelphia, Pennsylvania. The hospital is founded by Dr. Nathan Mossell for the welfare of the city's African American population.

1919 The Sterling Club, a social club for African Americans in Saint Paul, Minnesota is established.

1921 Former bootleg runner and NASCAR racer, Wendell Scott, is born in Danville Virginia. Scott is the first African American to win a major NASCAR race.

1926 Former Negro League baseball pitcher Bob Trice was born in Newton, Georgia. Trice was the first Black player for the Philadelphia Athletics

1928 Artist and community preservationist Joan Maynard is born in Brooklyn, New York. African American Maynard received many awards for her preservation work in the Weeksville community of Brooklyn.

1963 The March on Washington for Jobs and Freedom is held in Washington, D.C. On this date Martin Luther King, Jr. delivers his historic "I have a Dream" speech.

JAN
FEB
MAR
APR
MAY
JUN
JUL
AUG
SEP
OCT
NOV
DEC

 AUGUST 29

1778 1st Rhode Island Regiment of the Continental Army, a predominately Black unit, engages in its first confrontation in the Battle of Bloody Run Brook.

1917 Award-winning African American actress, Isabel Sanford is born in New York City. Sanford is the first African American to win an Emmy Award for lead role in a comedy series.

1920 Pioneering African American jazz saxophone player Charlie "Bird" Parker is born in Kansas City, Kansas. Parker's innovations in establishing bebop as a jazz style have cemented him as a jazz icon.

1920 Otis Boykin, African American inventor, is born in Dallas, Texas. Boykin is credited with inventing electronic resistors and a burglarproof cash register.

1924 African American blues singer Dinah Washington is born as Ruth Jones in Tuscaloosa, Alabama. Washington had many chart-topping hits in the 1950s and 60s, including "What a Difference a Day Made" and "Unforgettable." Dinah Washington was inducted in the Rock and Roll Hall of Fame in 1993.

1958 Singing mega-star Michael Jackson is born in Gary, Indiana. In 1983 Jackson made record history with the release of his "Thriller" album. It sold 45 million copies and contained seven top ten singles, including "Thriller," and "Beat It."

Michael Jackson arriving at a celebrity event, circa 1990

 ## AUGUST 30

1849 African American teacher and poet Henrietta Cordelia Ray is born in New York, New York. Her poem "Lincoln" was read at the dedication of the Emancipation Memorial in Washington, D. C.

1890 One of the Historical Black Colleges and Universities, Savannah State University is established in Savannah, Georgia.

1901 Newspaper editor and civil rights champion Roy Wilkins is born in Saint Louis, Missouri. Wilkins served as the executive director of the NAACP from 1955 to 1977.

1930 The first African American to

JAN
FEB
MAR
APR
MAY
JUN
JUL
AUG
SEP
OCT
NOV
DEC

host a prime-time TV show in the South, and civil rights activist, Xernoa Clayton is born in Muskogee, Oklahoma.

1943 African American dancer and actress Altovise (Gore) Davis is born in Charlotte, North Carolina. Davis, the wife of Sammy Davis, Jr., was the first to receive the NAACP's Black Woman of

Achievement Award for her positive example and charitable work.

2017 The case of Cherokee Nation v. Nash is decided, which allows people of African American decent who were living with the Cherokee Nation in 1866 and their descendants have the same rights as Cherokees, according to the treaty of 1866.

 ## AUGUST 31

1879 Livingstone College opens its doors to students. Located in Salisbury, North Carolina, it is one of the Historical Black Colleges and Universities.

1885 White author and playwright Eugene Dubose Heyward is

born in Charleston, South Carolina. He authored the play *Porgy*, the basis for the first American folk opera, *Porgy and Bess*, the story of an African American community on the docks of Charleston, South Carolina.

1907 California State Congressman Augustus "Gus" Hawkins is born in Shreveport, Louisiana. Hawkins was the first African American representative to serve in the California legislature. He served for 28 years.

. . . .

1936 Innovative African American educator Marva Knight Collins is born in Atmore, Alabama. Collins started the Westside Preparatory School in Chicago, Illinois, where she worked with low-income, low performing African American students with great success.

. . . .

1943 USS Harmon, the first United States Naval warship named after an African American, is christened. It is named after Leonard Roy Harmon for his heroic service during the Battle of Guadalcanal.

. . . .

1983 African American professional football player Larry Fitzgerald Jr. is born in Minneapolis, Minnesota. Fitzgerald played 17 seasons with the Arizona Cardinals.

. . . .

Larry Fitzgerald Jr. and Lauren Hobart attend the 2021 Footwear News Achievement Awards

SEPTEMBER 1

1773 Phillis Wheatly's book of poetry, *Poems on Various Subjects, Religious and Moral,* is published. It was the first American book of poetry written by a Black woman.

1862 The Penn Normal Industrial and Agricultural School opens in South Carolina. The Penn Center school, as it was known, was the first school for blacks on St. Helen Island in South Carolina.

1904 George Coleman Poage, becomes the first Black to medal in modern Olympic history. Mr. Poage took the bronze medal in the 200 meters and 400 meters.

1971 The Pittsburg Pirates made major league baseball history with the first all-Black major league baseball lineup. The players included: Rennie Stennett-2B, Gene Clines, Roberto Clemente, Willie Stargell, Manny Sanguillen, Dave Cash, Al Oliver, Jackie Hernandez, and Dock Ellis.

SEPTEMBER 2

1833 Oberlin College is established in Oberlin, Ohio. It is one of the first integrated private, coeducational schools.

1902 Rex Goreleigh, African American artist, was born in Peullym, Pennsylvania. Mr. Goreleigh is known for his paintings of Dean's Alley, Tomato Pickers, Misery, Quaker Bridge Road, and Sunflowers.

....

1922 Leigh Kamman, jazz ambassador, and host of the Minnesota Radio Program, is born in St. Louis, Minnesota. Mr. Kamman was a white radio announcer who promoted the African American art form of jazz.

....

1968 The Association of Black Psychologists is established in San Francisco, California.

The organization was formed to address the unique concerns of African American psychologists and their patients.

....

1972 The National Black Nurses Association is established in Cleveland, Ohio. The mission of the organization is to promote African American women in nursing and to provide for the health care of African Americans.

....

1977 The California African American Museum in Los Angeles is established by California Assembly Bill 420.

....

The California African American Museum (CAAM) at Exposition Park, Los Angeles

JAN
FEB
MAR
APR
MAY
JUN
JUL
AUG
SEP
OCT
NOV
DEC

SEPTEMBER 3

1783 Brichtown, Nova Scotia was founded. Brichtown was one of the largest free Black settlements in North America in colonial times.

1846 The American Missionary Association (AMA) is established. It was both an abolitionist and missionary society, but education was their primary goal.

1891 Annie Elizabeth Delany, dentist, and activist, is born in Raleigh, North Carolina. Ms. Delany was the second African American woman to practice dentistry in NY state. Annie and her elder sister, Sarah Delany, gained recognition as the subjects of a New York bestseller book, *Having Our Say: The Delany Sisters First 100 Years*.

1895 Influential African American lawyer Charles H. Houston is born in Washington, D. C. Mr. Houston is responsible for setting the foundation for the case of Brown v. Board of Education.

 # SEPTEMBER 4

1875 Knoxville College (KC) is dedicated in Knoxville, Tennessee. KC is one of the Historically Black Colleges and Universities.

1786 Jehu Jones, the first African American Lutheran minister, was born in Charleston, South Carolina. He founded St. Paul's Lutheran Church in Philadelphia, Pennsylvania.

1875 The Clinton Mississippi race riots occurred on this day when white Democrats attacked Republicans to coerce and intimidate Black Republicans and keep them from voting.

In the end over 50 African Americans were dead and scores of others fled to the federal garrison in Jackson for safety.

1908 Richard Wright, writer of socially relevant stories that encouraged conversations about race relations is born in Roxie, Mississippi. Mr. Wright is famous for his autobiographical work *Black Boy* and fictional novel *Native Son*.

SEPTEMBER 5

1830 Willam Allen, editor and abolitionist, is born. William Allen was a white American scholar who ran a school for emancipated slaves and editor of the first book of American Slave songs.

1901 Clarissa Scott Delaney, African American poet, is born in Tuskegee, Alabama. She is famous for her poems *Solace*, and *A Golden Afternoon in Germany*.

JAN
FEB
MAR
APR
MAY
JUN
JUL
AUG
SEP
OCT
NOV
DEC

1903 The Talented Tenth is an essay written by W.E.B. DuBois and published with a collection of essays called *the Negro Problem*. The term Talented Tenth originated among white northern liberals in 1896 but is associated with DuBois because of his most influential essay of the same name.

1965 The Watts Writers Workshop is established in Los Angeles, California. The workshop gave voices to urban Blacks to speak out on what they experienced during the Watts Riots.

SEPTEMBER 6

1841 The AME Church Review is published. The journal contents consist of articles on religion, history, and world events.

1883 Joel Augustus Rogers, anthropologist is born Negril, Jamaica. Rogers spent 50 years of his life investigating and reporting the achievements of historical and modern African people.

1910 Is the date of the opening of Holmes Avenue Elementary School in Los Angeles. It was the first school in Los Angeles to hire teachers without regard to color. Los Angeles first black teacher, Bessie Burke, started her career at Holmes Elementary

1988 The first Black Texas Ranger, Lee Roy Young, is hired. Ranger Young spent his 29-

year career working on cases throughout the state.

📄 SEPTEMBER 7

1859 John Merrick, businessman, is born in Clinton, North Carolina. Mr. Merrick established the North Carolina Mutual Insurance Company in 1898. N.C. Mutual had a staff of over 1200 and was the largest Black owned business by 1948.

1874 Classes for Longview Negro High School begin. It is noted as one of the earliest schools for Blacks in Texas.

1897 Newspaper editor and owner, Percy Green is born in Jackson, Mississippi. Jackson established the *Jackson Advocate*, the first American newspaper owned by and published for African Americans.

1918 Harold Amos, microbiologist, and professor, is born. Amos was known for his contribution to the research of bacterial metabolism, animal cell culture, and animal & bacterial virology. He was the first Black department head of Harvard Medical School.

1968 The first Miss Black America pageant is held in Philadelphia. Saundra William is the first to hold the coveted title.

Venus and Serena Williams in a doubles match at the 2013 Australian Open on January 22, 2013

 ## SEPTEMBER 8

1565 The One Drop Rule is acknowledged in St. Augustine, Florida. The rule states that any persons with any trace of African heritage cannot be classed as white. This rule became legitimate throughout the slave states.

1872 Ionia Rollin Whipper, obstetrician, is born in Beaufort, South Carolina. Dr. Whipper was employed with the United States Childrens Bureau to educate midwives in the South. Dr. Whipper and her supporters founded the Ionia R. Whipper Home for Unwed mothers in 1931.

1954 Ruby Bridges (Hall), educational activist, is born in Tylertown, Mississippi. She was the first child of African American heritage to attend William Frantz Elementary School in New Orleans, Louisiana. Hall now oversees the Ruby Bridges foundation, which promotes tolerance and inclusion.

2001 Venus and Serena Williams, sisters, were the first competitors to compose the first all-Black women's final at the tennis US open.

SEPTEMBER 9

1915 The Association for the Study of African American Life and History (ASALH) is established. The ASALH is the creation of Carter G. Woodson for education of individuals against racist and erroneous ideas about African American life and history.

1968 Arthur Ashe becomes the first African American man to win the U. S. Tennis Open singles championship.

1998 The Chicago Defender Building becomes an historical landmark. The Defender newspaper was a nationally recognized paper known for its editorials on civil rights issues.

2001 the University of Alabama's sorority and fraternity system remains segregated. U of A is the last college in the south where integration comes to U of A sororities and fraternities in 2003, when Gamma Phi Beta is the first sorority to accept a Black member.

2004 A lawsuit filed against the Cracker Barrel chain for

JAN
FEB
MAR
APR
MAY
JUN
JUL
AUG
SEP
OCT
NOV
DEC

discrimination by the NAACP is settled for 8.7 million. African American customers of the restaurant were subjected to racial slurs and served food taken from the trash.

 ## SEPTEMBER 10

1863 Jesse Edward Moorland, African American minister and administrator is born in Coldwater, Ohio. Moorland was instrumental in spreading the mission and purpose of the YMCA across the nation.

1880 Georgia (Camp) Johnson, Black playwright, poet, and patron of the arts is born in Marietta, Georgia. Johnson hosted a weekly forum in her Washington, D. C. home for many influential writers of the day.

1910 M. Moran Weston, minister, and social activist, is born in Tarboro, North Carolina. In addition to his Episcopal ministry duties, Weston served on many social, civic, and charity boards.

1928 Thornton Dial, Sr., African American steel worker and multimedia artist, is born in Emelle, Alabama. Dial worked all day as a steel worker and would create his art in the backyard after work. His work was brought to the attention of the art world in 1987.

1948 African American basketball player, coach and educational advocate, Bob Lanier, is born in Buffalo, New York. Lanier played with the Detroit Pistons and Milwaukee Bucks. He was known for his participation in the "Stay in School" and "Read to Achieve" programs.

1971 Attica prisoners rebel against the prison guards for the harsh situation in the prison. The mostly black prison population demanded better living conditions and educational opportunities. Seven days later the National Guard overtook the prison, killing 43 people in the process.

1982 World-renowned classical ballerina, dancer, and author, Misty Copeland, is born in Kansas City, Missouri. Copeland has won many awards for her dancing and was the first African American woman to be principal dancer in the distinguished American Ballet Theatre.

Misty Copeland as Ivy Smith/Miss Turnstyles in her debut performance of the Broadway musical *On The Town* in 2015

SEPTEMBER 11

1806 African American suffragist and abolitionist, Margaretta Foren, is born in Philadelphia, Pennsylvania. Foren, her mother, and sisters founded the Philadelphia Female Anti-Slavery Society.

1901 The hymn, "I'll Overcome Someday," which eventually became the theme song for the civil rights movement, "We Shall Overcome," is written by Dr. Charles Tindley.

1927 Older sister of Martin Luther King, Jr., Willie Christine King Farris, is born in Atlanta, Georgia. Farris was a teacher and member of many civic organizations. She is the author of the book *My Brother Martin: A Sister Remembers* *Growing Up with Rev. Dr. Martin Luther King Jr.*

1961 The Professional Golfers Association (PGA) of America Tour opens its membership to African American golfers.

1967 Minneapolis, Minnesota opens The City, Inc, a youth center, and alternative school for at risk youth.

1999 Serena Williams becomes the first African American women's tennis player to win the U. S. Open Tennis Championship since Althea Gibson in 1958.

2001 Twelve African American firefighters are among the 343 firefighters who lost their lives while

SEP

battling the attack on the World Trade Center in New York City.

 ## SEPTEMBER 12

1854 African American architect, Hazel Augustus, is born. He designed many homes, and most notably Payne Chapel A.M.E., and Tabernacle Baptist Church in West Palm Beach, Florida.

1858 A group of men, known as the Oberlin Wellington Rescuers, hide and help runaway slave, John Price get to Canada, putting their own lives and freedom in danger. Thirty-seven men were arrested for the act, only two served time of 20-60 days.

1865 Avery Normal Institute is established in Charleston, South Carolina. Avery operated as a vocational and college preparatory school for African Americans until 1954.

1913 Track and field star, Jesse Owens, is born in Danville, Alabama. Owens is noted for his four gold medals in the 1936 Olympics and Adolf Hitler's refusal to acknowledge his accomplishments at the games because he was Black. As a further insult, Pres. Franklin Roosevelt only invited white athletes to the White House.

1935 Richard Hunt, African American metal sculptor, and member of the

Smithsonian Board of Directors is born in Chicago, Illinois. He was the youngest artist to display his work at the 1962 Seattle World's Fair.

1936 Charles Crutchfield, Sr. obstetrician and gynecologist, is born in Jasper, Alabama. He is the first African American to open an ob/gyn practice in Minnesota. Crutchfield delivered over 9000 babies during his career.

1944 Barry White, African American soul singer, is born in 1944. His husky voice brought him fame with the songs "Never, Never, Gonna Give you Up," and Can't Get Enough of Your Love, Babe."

 # SEPTEMBER 13

1881 Lewis Latimer, an African American associate of Thomas Edison, receives a patent for his improvements to the carbon filament in the electric lightbulb.

1885 Influential philosopher, Alain Locke is born in Philadelphia, Pennsylvania. Locke worked to define and establish the Harlem Renaissance and was the first Black to receive a Rhodes Scholarship to study at the University of Oxford in England.

1886 The Delaware Conference is established in Princess Anne, Maryland as one of the Historically

Black Universities and Colleges. After several name changes, it is now operated as University of Maryland Eastern Shore.

1934 Henry Sampson, Jr., engineer, inventor, and Black movie historian is born in Jackson, Mississippi. Sampson was the first African American to receive his Ph.D. in Nuclear engineering and created improved rocket propellants.

1948 The African American stage, and TV performer, Nell Carter is born in Birmingham, Alabama. She won a Tony Award for her work in the play *Ain't Misbehavin'* and played the lead character Nell Harper in the long-running TV show "Gimme a Break!"

1953 The Philadelphia Athletics sign their first African American player, pitcher, Bob Trice.

2000 James Perkins becomes the first African American mayor of Selma, Alabama.

📑 SEPTEMBER 14

1865 One of many Black post-Civil War towns, Kendelton, Texas is established by former slaves from the area.

1867 The Brooklyn Colored School opens in Oakland California. It is a school for African American children in the towns of both Oakland and Brooklyn.

JAN
FEB
MAR
APR
MAY
JUN
JUL
AUG
SEP
OCT
NOV
DEC

1874 The Battle of Liberty Place in New Orleans, Louisiana begins. Between three and five thousand members of the White League, primarily former Confederate soldiers, attacked and held the government buildings for three days until Pres. Grant sent in federal troops to break up the mob and restore the elected government.

1921 Constance Baker Motley, lawyer, judge, and politician is born in New Haven, Connecticut. Motley is the first African American to hold New York senate seat and is the first to be appointed to a federal judgeship.

1928 The Hotel Sommerville, currently the Dunbar Hotel, in Los Angeles opens. The hotel was built by John Sommerville, a prominent dentist and businessman, to accommodate the needs of Blacks in Los Angeles.

1964 Elaine Weddington Steward, sports lawyer and administrator, is born in New York, New York. As assistant manager of the Boston Red Socks, she was the first African American woman to work as a professional baseball executive and has received many awards and accolades.

1990 For the first time in major league baseball, a father and son hit back-to-back homeruns while on the same Seattle Mariners team. African Americans Ken Griffey, Sr. and Ken Griffey, Jr. are also the first father and son to play on the same professional baseball team.

Ken Griffey Jr. speaks at BottleRock in 2019

 # SEPTEMBER 15

1799 Free-born African American abolitionist, Nancy Garder Prince is born in Newburyport, Massachusetts.

1821 Spain grants the Republic of Costa Rica independence.

1844 Cathay Williams, Buffalo Soldier, is born in Independence, MO. After the Civil War, she enlisted in the 38th US. Infantry (Buffalo soldier Unit) as a man, William Cathay.

Cathay Williams was the only woman known to serve as a Buffalo soldier.

1847 Dentist, professor, and inventor, George Grant is born in Oswego, New York. Grant was the first African American professor at Harvard and was granted a patent for his golf tee.

1890 African American Claude McKay, author of *Home to Harlem*, is

JAN
FEB
MAR
APR
MAY
JUN
JUL
AUG
SEP
OCT
NOV
DEC

born in Clarendon Parish, Jamaica.

1943 World-famous African American fashion designer, Stephen Burrows is born in Newark, New Jersey. He is known for his color-block fashions and was a popular designer for the stars.

1980 Lewis Place in Saint Louis, Missouri becomes a National Landmark. It was the center of the Supreme Court Case of Shelly v. Kraemer, that alleged that rules against people of color living in certain areas is not against the law, such rules could not be upheld in court.

 # SEPTEMBER 16

1920 Cozelle Breedlove, African American coach, teacher, and educational advocate, is born in Minneapolis, Minnesota. Breedlove dedicated his life to the nurturing and support of the Phyllis Wheatly House.

1925 Jazz and blues guitar legend, B.B. King is born near Itta Bene, Mississippi. During his lifetime King received fifteen Grammy Awards and released over fifty albums.

1943 Author James McPherson is born in Savannah, Georgia. McPherson is the first African American to win a Pulitzer Prize for fiction.

1950 Henry Gates, Jr., author, educator, and advocate for

African American literature, is born in Keser, West Virginia.

2002 The Key West African cemetery is re-dedicated and consecrated in Key West, Florida.

2011 The first wholly-Black owned airline in South Africa, Santaco Airlines is established.

 ## SEPTEMBER 17

1808 Juliette Gaudin, Afro Cuban nun and educator is born in Cuba. Catholic Sis. Juliette and another sister, Henriette Delille, form The Sisters of the Holy Family, dedicated to helping the orphans, poor, and elderly.

1866 Lincoln University of Missouri is established in Jefferson City. Originally known as the Lincoln Institute, it is one of the Historically Black Colleges and Universities.

1879 Black baseball player, manager and organizer of the Negro National League, Andrew "Rube" Foster, is born in Calvert, Texas.

1900 Dr. Lena Edwards, African American doctor, and humanitarian, is born in Washington, D. C. She received the Presidential Medal of Freedom from Pres. Lyndon Johnson for her work in establishing the Guadeloupe Maternity Clinic in Hereford, Texas.

JAN
FEB
MAR
APR
MAY
JUN
JUL
AUG
SEP
OCT
NOV
DEC

1953 The Chicago Cubs sign Gene Baker and Ernie Banks from the Negro League Kansas City Monarchs, integrating the Cubs for the first time.

1962 Actor Rex Ingram becomes the first African American cast in a daytime drama series.

1983 Vanessa Williams becomes the first African American to be crowned Miss America.

 ## SEPTEMBER 18

1850 The Fugitive Slave Act is signed. This law required for escaped slaves from the south and caught in a free state to be returned to their former masters.

1895 African American activist Booker T. Washington makes the Atlanta Compromise speech in Atlanta. In his address he made the following statement, "In all things that are purely social, we can be as separate as the fingers, yet on as the hand in all things essential to mutual progress."

1905 Black actor and comedian, Eddie Anderson, is born in Oakland, California. Anderson appeared in some of the most recognizable films of the day including, *Man About Town*, and *Love Thy Neighbor* both with Jack Benny, as well as *Gone with the Wind*, and *Birth of the Blues*.

1935 The Norfolk Unit of Virginia

State University, one of the Historically Black Colleges and Universities, is established in Norfolk, Virginia.

....

1951 African American neurosurgeon and administer Ben Carson is born in Detroit, Michigan. Carson's extraordinary surgical skills were made famous when he separated conjoined twins in 1997.

....

1954 Dennis Johnson, African American basketball player and coach, was born in San Pedro, California. He played for the Seattle Supersonics, Phoenix Suns, and Boston Celtics.

....

1972 Art Williams is the first African American to umpire a National League baseball game at San Diego Stadium.

....

 ## SEPTEMBER 19

1797 Sojourner Truth, African American former slave, abolitionist, and suffragist is born in Hurley, New York. Sojourner Truth was known as a powerful and persuasive speaker in the cause of emancipation.

....

1835 Free-born African American preacher and abolitionist, Theodore Miller is born in New York, New York.

....

1838 Susan (Smith) Vashon, African American teacher and social leader was born in Boston,

JAN
FEB
MAR
APR
MAY
JUN
JUL
AUG
SEP
OCT
NOV
DEC

Massachusetts. Vashon was directly involved with fund raising for the care of soldiers from the Civil War, and the relief of refugees from the South.

1845 Black Canadian rancher and cowboy John Ware is born near Georgetown, South Carolina. His contributions to agriculture and cattle ranching in the Alberta region have led him to become a Canadian legend.

1883 The Haines Normal and Industrial Institute opens in Augusta, Georgia as a school for blacks during Reconstruction.

1889 African American teacher Sarah Delany is born. Sarah and her sister Elizabeth Delany were the subjects of the book, *Having Our Say; The Delany Sisters' First 100 Years."* Sarah lived to be 109.

1934 African American television and screen actor Lloyd Haynes is born in South Bend, Indiana. He is best known for his role as teacher Pete Dixon on the popular 1960s TV show, *Room 222.*

Harriet Tubman Square in Boston, Massachusetts

SEPTEMBER 20

1830 The first National Negro Convention Meets in Philadelphia, Pennsylvania in answer to the question of sixteen-year-old Hezekiel Grice. His question was, should free blacks be emigrating to Canada? After writing to several influential free Blacks, the convention was an attempt to answer it.

1831 The Philadelphia, Pennsylvania Female Literary Association is established by Sarah Mapps Douglas. The Association was a social group where African American women could support the worthy causes of the day.

1853 Harriet Tubman begins working with the Underground Railroad. She assisted over 300 slaves in their journey to freedom.

1881 With a common goal of voting rights of women and Blacks, The Minnesota Woman Suffrage Association is established.

1915 Jewish-American civil rights activist and mathematician Lee Lorch is born. Lorch lost several college teaching positions due to his support of the rights of African Americans. He eventually moved to Canada to find steady employment.

1918 Actor, musician, and announcer, Gordon Heath is born in New York City. Heath was the first

African American staff announcer for a major U.S. radio station in 1945.

1958 Martin Luther King, Jr. is injured in an assassination attempt while signing his book, *Stride Toward Freedom* in New York City.

1968 Anthony "Van" Jones, African American lawyer and activist is born in Jackson, Tennessee. Jones was instrumental in the founding of numerous social organizations including the Ella Baker Center for Human Rights, Color of Change, and Green for All.

SEPTEMBER 21

1891 John W. Hardrick, African American painter, is born in Indianapolis, Indiana. Hardrick received great acclaim for his paintings of African Americans, and landscapes.

1897 A "gentleman flyer," Hubert Julian is born in Trinidad. He was the first Black man to fly from coast-to-coast.

1898 African American labor activist, nurse, and welder, Frances Albrier is born in Mount Vernon, New York. After attending the University of California, Berkeley to become a nurse, and a voice for the African American community in Berkeley and Oakland.

1905 Former slave and barber, Alonzo Herndon establishes the Atlanta Life

Insurance Company. The company now has office in 17 states and is one of the largest African American businesses in the U. S.

1947 Archbishop Joseph Ritter insists that the Catholic schools in Saint Louis, Missouri become integrated.

1981 The Central American country of Belize receives independence from Britain.

2002 Brenda Knight becomes the first African American woman to be elected to the Association of Community Colleges and Trustees.

SEPTEMBER 22

1863 The 8th United States Colored Infantry is established by the Bureau of Colored Troops in Philadelphia, Pennsylvania.

1904 The town of Boley, Oklahoma is established in central Oklahoma. Booker T. Washington described it as "the most enterprising, and in many ways the most interesting of the Negro towns in the U. S."

1921 Betty Charbonnet Reid Soskin, African American record store owner and National Park Ranger, is born in Detroit, Michigan. Soskin was influential in creating The Rosie, the Riveter/World War II Home Front National Historical Park in Richmond, California. She became a National

Park interpreter at the museum at the age of 85.

1941 African American social activist and minister, Jeremiah Wright is born in Philadelphia, Pennsylvania. Wright led the Trinity United Church of Christ in Chicago from 250 members in 1972 to 6000 members by 2008.

1950 Ralph Bunche becomes the first Black person to receive the Nobel Peace Prize. He received the award for his work in establishing armistice agreements between Israel and its neighbors, Egypt, Jordan, Lebanon, and Syria.

1966 David Adjaye, Black Ghanaian-British architect is born in Tanzania. Adjaye is the architect who created the National Museum of African American History and Culture in Washington, D. C.

The National Museum of African American History and Culture located on the National Mall

SEPTEMBER 23

1863 Mary Church Terrell, social activist and first president of the National Association of Colored Women, is born in Memphis, Tennessee.

1884 Judy W. Reed receives a patent for her dough kneader and roller.

1905 One of the first libraries for African Americans, the Western Library of Louisville, Kentucky opens.

1926 Pioneering African American saxophonist, John Coltrane is born in Hamlet, North Carolina. Coltrane was a major contributor to the bebop style of jazz.

1930 One of the most universally recognized singers of the 1960s and 70s, Ray Charles is born in Albany, Georgia. Blind since the age of six, Charles was one of the first to blend gospel and blues with songs such as, "What'd I Say," and "Georgia on my Mind."

1931 Industrial designer Charles Harrison is born in Louisiana. Harrison is the first African American to receive the Lifetime Achievement National Design Award.

1942 Wendell Gunn, the first African American to integrate into the University of North Alabama, was born in Tuscumbia, Alabama.

SEPTEMBER 24

1825 Member of the American Anti-Slavery Society and National Association of Colored Women Clubs, Frances Ellen Watkins Harper is born in Baltimore, Maryland. Harper was the first African American woman to publish a short story.

1878 The patent for a unique library table is granted to African American William Davis, Jr. of New York, New York.

1888 An HBCU, St. Paule's Normal and Industrial School of Virginia, currently St. Paul's College, is established in Lawrenceville. Virginia.

1924 Daniel Davis, African American boxer, and social advocate is born in Minneapolis, Minnesota.

1924 African American actress of stage, screen, and television, Theresa Merritt is born in Emporia, Virginia. She is best remembered for her role in "That's My Mama," and as Aunt Em in the film *The Wiz*."

1931 Cardiss Collins, the first African American woman to serve as a congresswoman from Illinois, is born in St. Louis, Missouri.

1936 Research chemist, William Jackson, is born in Birmingham, Alabama. Jackson was one of the co-founders of National Organization for the Professional

Advancement of Black Chemists and Chemical Engineers.

1957 President Dwight Eisenhower signs the executive order to provide nine African American students a U. S. Army escort to Little Rock, Arkansas' Central High School.

2016 The National Museum of African American History and Culture opens in Washington, D. C.

 # SEPTEMBER 25

1861 The first Blacks are admitted to the Union Navy.

1911 Eric Williams, Afro Caribbean author, and politician is born in Trinidad. Williams was Prime Minister of Trinidad and Tobago from 1962-1981.

1919 African American Naval hero Charles French is born in Foreman, Arkansas. French received a letter of commendation for his efforts in rescuing 15 other sailors near Guadalcanal.

1952 Pamela Alexander, African American lawyer, and judge is born in Minneapolis, Minnesota. She has won numerous awards and recognitions for her community service.

1968 African American actor and rapper Will Smith is born in West Philadelphia, Pennsylvania. Smith is known for "The Fresh

Prince of Bel-Air," and a
wide variety of movies.

1983 Singer, actor,
and director Donald
Glover is born at
Edwards Airforce Base
in California. He has
appeared in the movies
The Martian, *Spider-
Man: Homecoming*,

and *Solo: A Star Wars
Story*.

2009 The 1941 film
The Blood of Jesus, a
Black production, is
added to the Library
of Congress' Nation
Film Registry as
culturally significant.

SEPTEMBER 26

1795 Alexander
Twilight, Vermont state
legislator and school
principal, is born in
Corinth, Vermont.
Twilight was the first
African American to
graduate from an
American college.

1929 African
American physicist and
Olympic silver medalist,
Meredith Gourdine is
born in Newark, New
Jersey. Gourdine won
the silver medal for
the long jump in the
1952 Olympics. As a

physicist, he researched
the effects of electric
fields on gases.

1929 Ida Stephens
Owens, African
American biophysicist,
is born in Newark,
New Jersey. She was a
pioneer in the field of
genetics.

1936 Anti-apartheid
activist and politician,
Winnie Madikizela-
Mandela is born
in Cape Province,
South Africa. She was
the wife of Nelson

Mandela and was a member of the South African Parliament.

1937 African American microbiologist and community activist, Edith Amos Hambie is born in Decatur, Georgia. Hambie worked at the Centers for Disease Control for 44 years, gaining many honors and recognitions.

1952 Kendall School for the Deaf in Washington, D. C. opens its doors to African American students on its campus for the first time.

1981 African American Tennis phenom Serena Williams is born in Saginaw, Michigan. She is the top grossing women's tennis player of all time (as of 2022).

 # SEPTEMBER 27

1822 The first African American Senator, Hiram Revels, is born in Fayetteville, North Carolina.

1862 In what came to be the 73rd Regiment Infantry U. S. Colored Troops for the Union Army, The First Louisiana Native Guard is formed in New Orleans, Louisiana.

1915 The Sisters of the Blessed Sacrament for Indians and Colored People of Louisiana, a high school, opens in New Orleans. The school later becomes Xavier University, one of the Historically Black Colleges and Universities.

JAN
FEB
MAR
APR
MAY
JUN
JUL
AUG
SEP
OCT
NOV
DEC

1935 The first woman pitcher in the Negro Leagues, Mame "Peanut" Johnson is born in Ridgeway, South Carolina. Hank Aaron was one of her teammates on the Indianapolis Clowns.

1936 Don Cornelius, the host of the TV show *Soul Train*, is born in Chicago, Illinois. Soul Train was created to showcase the talents and songs of Black singers and musicians.

1947 The African American magazine Sepia is established highlighting the achievements of African Americans.

2003 A raid on a slave labor camp in Nigeria rescues 116 Black African boys working at a granite quarry.

 # SEPTEMBER 28

1890 The Alabama Penny Savings Bank, the first bank for and run by African Americans in Alabama, opens for business.

1892 The Salter Industrial Academy, currently Winston-Salem State University (WSSU), is established in Winston-Salem, North Carolina. WSSU is one of the Historically Black Colleges and Universities.

1892 Mary Holmes College (MHC), previously Mary Holmes Seminary, is established in Jackson, Mississippi. MHC is one of the HBCUs.

1912 "Memphis Blues," credited as the song that began the Blues, was released in Memphis, Tennessee by W. C. Handy.

1947 Harold Dow, the first African American television news journalist in Nebraska, is born in Hackensack, New Jersey.

1857 World-renowned African American psychologist Beverly Daniel Tatum is born in Tallahassee. She is known for the book *Why are All the Black Kids Sitting Together in the Cafeteria? And Other Conversations About Race.*

1962 The Supreme Court rules for James Meridith in the case of Meridith v. Fair. The suit alleged that the University of Mississippi prevented Meridith's enrollment because he was African American.

1976 Lou Bellamy establishes the Penumbra Theater Company to provide a public outlet for African American expression through theater in St. Paul, Minnesota.

1990 Kansas City, Missouri opens the Negro Leagues Baseball Museum.

 # SEPTEMBER 29

1887 African American Mary Kenner receives a patent for her Shower Back Washer.

JAN
FEB
MAR
APR
MAY
JUN
JUL
AUG
SEP
OCT
NOV
DEC

1909 Winner of two gold medals at the 1932 Olympics, Eddie Tolan, is born in Denver, Colorado. Tolan is the first African American to win two gold medals in the same Olympics.

1920 The first African American nurse in the Regular Army Nurse Corps, Nancy Leftenant, is born in Goose Creek, South Carolina.

1926 Chuck Cooper, the first African American signed by a National Basketball League team, is born in Pittsburgh, Pennsylvania.

1933 The first African American

mayor of Opelousas, Louisiana, John Joseph was born in Plaisance, Louisiana.

1942 The U. S. Booker T. Washington, the first U. S. merchant ship named for an African American, is launched in Wilmington, Delaware. It was also the first merchant ship to be captained by an African American, Hugh Mulzac.

1955 Gwen Ifill, African American television news journalist, is born in Queens, New York. She was the senior correspondent on the NewsHour with Jim Lehrer on PBS.

 ## SEPTEMBER 30

1872 Africatown, Alabama is established by a group of 32 West Africans in the last shipment of illegal slaves. The citizens of Africatown held to their African culture and language well into the 20th century.

1887 Florida Agricultural and Mechanical College, now known as Florida Agricultural and Mechanical University, is established in Tallahassee, Florida. Florida A&M is one of the HBCUs.

1890 Irene West, African American civil rights activist and educator is born in Perry County, Alabama.

1919 When white residents fell threatened by African American sharecroppers' attempt to join the Progressive Farmers and Household Union of America a race riot breaks out in Elaine, Arkansas.

1935 Recipient of the Lifetime Achievement Award from the Academy of Recording Arts and Sciences, Johnny Mathis is born in Gilmer, Texas. Some of his most popular songs include, "Chances Are," "It's Not for Me to Say," and "Too Much, Too Little, Too Late."

1940 Harry Jerome, Olympic sprinter, and Canadian social activist is born in Prince Albert, Saskatchewan, Canada.

2004 The Ertegun Jazz Hall of Fame is dedicated as part of the Lincoln Center for the Performing Arts. Nesuhi Ertegun was one of the founders of Atlantic Records, which was instrumental in the development of jazz in the United States.

JAN
FEB
MAR
APR
MAY
JUN
JUL
AUG
SEP
OCT
NOV
DEC

JAN
FEB
MAR
APR
MAY
JUN
JUL
AUG
SEP
OCT
NOV
DEC

 # OCTOBER 1

1750 Peter Salem, soldier, and patriot, is born a slave in Framingham, Massachusetts As a freed Black man, he became one of the minutemen heroes of the American Revolutionary War.

1846 Theo Allain, politician, is born a slave in Baton Rouge Parish, Louisiana. Allain was a member of Louisiana State Legislature championing for the rights and living conditions of the newly freed Blacks.

1866 Shorter College is established. The AME Church founded the college under the name of Bethel Institute. It is a historically Black private college that offered bachelor's degrees up until 1955.

1897 Florence Powell, librarian, and teacher, is born in Wilkinsburg, PA. After graduating from Carnegie Library School and some controversy she was the first Black woman to receive a professional degree in library science in the United States.

 # OCTOBER 2

1672 Built with the slave labor of African and Native Americans, construction on the

Castillo De San Marcos Fort begins. The fort is built to protect the interests of Spain in the area and is currently being maintained as a National Monument by the National Park Service.

1800 Nat Turner, slave, and abolitionist, is born in Southampton County, Virginia. Turner was the leader of the Southampton Insurrection.

1850 Sarah Goode, inventor, and former slave is born in Toledo, Ohio. Ms. Goode is known for her invention of the cabinet bed.

1897 George Washington Bright, the first Black firefighter in Los Angeles is hired.

1916 Paul Laurence Dunbar High School in Washington, D. C. opens a new campus.

It was the first high school for African American youth when it was originally established in 1870.

1937 African American defense lawyer best known for his defense of O.J. Simpson, Johnnie Cochran, is born in Shreveport, Louisiana.

1967 Thurgood Marshall is sworn in as the first black judge on the United States Supreme Court. Appointed by President Lyndon B. Johnson, Justice Marshall was on the forefront of the civil rights movement.

1971 The Soul Train African American dance program aired on television. It was the longest first run nationally syndicated program in American television history.

Mary McLeod Bethune, right, founder of the National Council of Negro Women, with Dorothy Height, who became the organization's director in 1957

 # OCTOBER 3

1881 Dudley Woodward, mathematician, is born Woodward is the second black man to receive a Ph.D. in Mathematics. Dr. Woodward is responsible for establishing the MS degree program at Howard University.

1904 Bethune-Cookman University is founded. It is the only historical black college founded by a black woman, Mary Mcleod Bethune. Originally Daytona Literary and Industrial Training School for Negro Girls, it merged with Cookman Institute for boys to become Bethune-Cookman University.

1924 The first game of the World Series of the Negro Leagues, dubbed the "Colored World Series," was played in National League Park in Philadelphia, Pennsylvania. The Kansas City Monarchs beat the Hilldales of Darby, Pennsylvania, 6 to 2.

JAN
FEB
MAR
APR
MAY
JUN
JUL
AUG
SEP

OCT
NOV
DEC

1965 President Lyndon Johnson signed, The Immigration and Nationality Act. The bill eliminates restrictions on visas with a per country-of-origin quota. In the past, the law excluded Asians and Africans and preferred northern and western Europeans over eastern and southern Europeans.

OCTOBER 4

1864 The National Equal Rights League (NERL) is founded at the National Conference of Colored Men in Syracuse, New York. The league mission is to promote everything that encourages a well ordered and dignified life for African Americans. NERL is the oldest human rights organization in the United States.

1877 The town of Nicodemus is established in Kansas. It was the first rural settlement for blacks after the Civil War and became the largest black colony in America.

1943 H "Rap" Brown, Black Panther and SNCC activist, is born in Baton Rouge, Louisiana. He was a member of the Nonviolent Action Group (NAG) and the director of Student Nonviolent Coordinating Committee (SNCC). Brown was known for eloquence in public speaking which earned him the title of "Rap."

2003 The African Burial Ground is

JAN
FEB
MAR
APR
MAY
JUN
JUL
AUG
SEP
OCT
NOV
DEC

re-established and re-consecrated in New York City. The burial ground is a six-acre

cemetery that was used for slaves that were not buried in the church cemetery

 # OCTOBER 5

1881 Tim Brymn, Bandleader is born in Kinston, North Carolina. His Black Devils orchestra, attached to the 350th Field Artillery, played at the WWI Peace Talks in Paris, France.

1862 The First Baptist Church of Georgetown is Founded. It is the oldest and most recognized church in the Washington, D.C. area. Reverend Sandy Alexander, a former slave, moved to Georgetown in 1856 to start a Baptist church and was able to build up a large congregation.

Alexander was the pastor of that church for 37 years which has become part of Washington, D.C. history.

1903 The Charleston Dance is celebrated on this day. The dance originated with the Ashanti people of Africa. It was modified during slavery by Blacks living on a small island near Charleston, South Carolina. It gained worldwide popularity during the rag-time jazz period.

1916 William Stetson Kennedy, white southern aristocrat, and human rights activist is born in Jacksonville, Florida. He was best known for exposing Klu Klux Klan secrets and rituals.

OCTOBER 6

1871 The Fisk Jubilee Singers are founded. The group of emancipated Slaves raised $50,000 for Fisk University by touring the United States and Europe, introducing gospel music and Black folk music to the world.

1917 Fannie Lou Hamer, civil rights activist, is born in Montgomery County, Mississippi. Ms. Hamer became a national symbol for poor southern blacks in the civil rights movement when she attempted to vote and was forced from her home with her family.

1949 Lonnie G. Johnson, inventor, aerospace engineer, and mathematician is born in Mobile, Alabama. After distinguished service in the Air Force, Johnson joined NASA's Jet Propulsion Laboratory where he contributed to work on the Galileo, Jupiter probe and Mars Observer project.

1964 The Campaign Against Racial Discrimination (CARD) is founded in London, England. While Martin Luther King, Jr. was in London he met with a group which formed committee lobby for race legislation in England.

Desmond Tutu at Hay-On-Wye in 2009

 # OCTOBER 7

1886 Slavery is ended in Cuba by royal decree. The indigenous people provided the initial supply of slave labor in the sugar industry until they were wiped-out due to the working conditions and other slaves were brought in to replace them.

1897 Elijah Muhammad, Nation of Islam Leader, is born in Sandersville, Georgia. Muhammad was the leader of a Black separatist religious movement known as the Nation of Islam or as Black Muslims.

1912 Charleszetta Waddles, African American community activist, is born in St. Louis, Missouri. Waddles established a thriving service agency called the Perpetual Mission to serve the lower income communities of Detroit, Michigan. The Perpetual Mission was privately funded and staffed by volunteers.

1931 Desmond Tutu, Anglican Archbishop, is born. Desmond Tutu is the first Black South African Anglican Archbishop to be elected and ordained in Cape Town, South Africa. Tutu was awarded the Gandhi Peace Prize in February of 2007.

 # OCTOBER 8

1898 African American musician, and businessman Clarence Williams is born in Plaquemine, Louisiana. Williams was an early proponent of jazz and its musical form.

1901 Harlem New York YMCA is established. The Black YMCA was the result of the organizations official stance on segregation and served the largest African American membership in the United States.

1986 Wole Soyinka, is the first black to win the Nobel Prize in Literature. Soyinka's 1996 work, *The Open Sore of a Continent*, is a commentary on the leadership crisis in Africa.

1993 Bubba Wallace Jr., NASCAR Driver, and Activist is born in Mobile, Alabama. Wallace became the second African American to win the NASCAR Cup and has been a vocal supporter of the Black Lives Matter Movement.

JAN
FEB
MAR
APR
MAY
JUN
JUL
AUG
SEP
OCT
NOV
DEC

OCTOBER 9

1842 Saint Augustine Catholic Church is established in New Orleans, Louisiana. Since the founding of the church, it has welcomed both slaves and free peoples to worship, making it the most integrated congregation in the country at that time.

1895 Eugene Bullard, African American aviator, is born in Columbus, GA. In Paris Bullard joined the French Foreign Legion and was awarded the Croix de Guerre. Bullard transferred to the Lafayette Flying Corps in the French Aeronautique Militaire.

1932 African American Aviators, Thomas Allen and James Banning, complete the first transcontinental flight.

2009 United States President Barack Obama is awarded the Nobel Peace Prize. The President achieved this award for his stellar efforts to strengthen international diplomacy and cooperation between peoples.

 # OCTOBER 10

1899 African American Issac R. Johnson receives a patent for a bicycle frame.

1917 Thelonious Monk, bebop jazz musician, is born in Rocky Mount, NC. Monk, known as the high priest of bebop, is a jazz pianist and is famous for his musical pieces Round Midnight, Ruby, My Dear, and Straight No Chaser.

....

1927 Hazel Johnson-Brown, Nurse and Officer, was born on this day in West Chester, PA. Johnson-Brown became the first Black female General in the United States Army.

....

1935 The first Broadway folk opera to feature a story about the lives of African Americans, *Porgy and Bess*, opens on Broadway. Many African Americans felt it reinforced negative stereotypes of Black communities.

....

 # OCTOBER 11

1825 Afro Brazilian author and educator, Maria Firmina dos Reis, is born in São Luis, Maranhão, Brazil. She is the author of *Úrsula*, a story of slavery in Brazil.

....

1882 Robert Dett, pianist, arranger, and composer is born in Drummondville, Ontario, Canada. Dett is considered an important contributor to the introduction of African American spirituals and folk songs to the public.

....

1887 The State Normal school for Colored Persons

opens in Frankfort, Kentucky. It is now known as Kentucky State University. KSU is one of the Historically Black Colleges and Universities.

1907 African American tap dancer, Clayton Bates, is born in Fountain Inn, South Carolina. Bates lost his leg in a farming accident at the age of 12 but learned to dance with a pegleg. He became a world-renowned dancer throughout the 1930s, 40s, and 50s.

1919 Art Blakey, African American jazz pianist, drummer, and bandleader, is born in Pittsburgh, Pennsylvania. Blakey was a sought-after drummer and played with the likes of Billy Eckstine, Charlie Parker, Thelonious Monk, and Miles Davis.

1924 Malvin Whitfield, African American Olympic athlete and Tuskegee Airman is born in Bay City, Texas. Whitfield won the Olympic gold medal for the 800m in 1948 and 1952.

1928 The first African American to achieve the rank of four-star general, Roscoe Robinson, Jr., is born in St. Louis, Missouri.

1936 African American jazz drummer Billy Higgins is born in Los Angeles, California. He played with many of the popular jazz ensembles of his day.

OCTOBER 12

1883 African American physicist Elmer Imes is born in Memphis, Tennessee. Imes is known for his pioneering work in Quantum Theory.

1906 Jay Saunders Redding, author, and educator was born in Wilmington, Delaware. He was the first African American member of the faculty at Brown University.

1908 Ann Lane Petry, author, was born in Seabrook, Connecticut. Her first book *The Street* became the first book written by an African American woman to sell more than a million copies.

1916 African American playwright and author, Alice Childress, is born in Charleston, South Carolina. Childress' stories focus on the hope and optimism of the African American people.

1919 African American WWII hero, Dorie Miller is born in Waco, Texas. Miller was awarded the Navy Cross for his heroic actions during the Japanese bombing of Pearl Harbor on December 7, 1941. Two U. S. naval ships bear his name, the USS Miller, and the USS Doris Miller.

1932 Richard "Dick" Gregory, an African American comedian, and Civil Rights activist, is born in St. Louis, Missouri.

JAN
FEB
MAR
APR
MAY
JUN
JUL
AUG
SEP
OCT
NOV
DEC

JAN
FEB
MAR
APR
MAY
JUN
JUL
AUG
SEP

OCT
NOV
DEC

In his later years he was known for his critical opinions of the American government.

2001 Ghanaian Kofi Annan, Secretary- General of the United Nations (UN), and the UN organization are awarded the 2001 Nobel Peace Prize for their contributions to a more peaceful world.

Kofi Annan meets the President of the Hellenic Republic, Prokopis Pavlopoulos, in Athens, Greece, in 2017

OCTOBER 13

1898 Lawyer and judge, Raymond Alexander is born in Philadelphia, Pennsylvania. Alexander was to become the first African American to sit on the Common Pleas Court in Philadelphia.

1898 Edith Spurlock Sampson, community advocate and judge, is born in Pittsburgh, Pennsylvania. Sampson became the first African American woman delegate to the United Nations, and first African American woman elected to a municipal court.

1902 Arna Bontemps, African American poet, author, and librarian is born in Alexandria, Louisiana. Bontemps won many awards for his poetry, including from the magazines *The Crisis*, and *Opportunity*.

1909 One of the most technically accurate jazz pianists of all time, African American Art Tatum, is born in Toledo, Ohio. Tatum was known for his unique rapid runs that made his music easily recognizable.

1914 African American Garrett Morgan is granted a patent for his breathing device, a precursor to the gas mask.

1924 African American comedian, Nipsey Russell, is born in Atlanta, Georgia. Russell was well known for his appearances on many celebrity game shows.

1926 Jesse L. Brown, the first African American Navy pilot, is born in Hattiesburg, Mississippi. The naval ship USS Jesse L Brown was commissioned in his honor after being shot down during the Korean war.

 # OCTOBER 14

1813 Free Black man and abolitionist, Samuel Burris, is born in Delaware. Burris was a conductor on the Underground Railroad to help slaves on their way to freedom.

JAN
FEB
MAR
APR
MAY
JUN
JUL
AUG
SEP
OCT
NOV
DEC

JAN
FEB
MAR
APR
MAY
JUN
JUL
AUG
SEP
OCT
NOV
DEC

1889 One of the first cases to address the issue of desegregation in public schools, Wysinger v. Crookshank is filed with the Supreme Court of California.

1896 Oscar Charleston, center fielder for several of the Negro League baseball teams, is born in Indianapolis. Indiana. He was the only Black player in the Manila League in 1914, while he was stationed in the Philippines during WWI.

1916 Rutgers football team sidelined their best player, African American Paul Robeson, when Virginia's Washington and Lee College refused to take the field with a Black player. It was the first and last time Rutgers would back down from that challenge.

1927 African American actress and nightclub performer, Joyce Bryant, is born in Oakland, California. In 1956 Bryant gave up her profitable career to be an advocate for the poor and needy in the South.

1958 Mamie Parker, environmentalist, wildlife biologist, and administrator, is born in Wilmot, Arkansas. Parker was the first African American Regional Director of the U. S. Fish and Wildlife Service.

1964 Martin Luther King, Jr. receives the Nobel Peace Prize for his methods of nonviolent protest.

2021 The Rolling Stones retire the song "Brown Sugar" for its insensitive and derogatory lyrics.

OCTOBER 15

1885 Morris Brown College opens its doors for the first time in Atlanta, Georgia. MBC was established by the AME Church and is one of the Historically Black Colleges and Universities.

1917 Six hundred thirty-nine African American officers graduate from Fort Des Moines military school in preparation for World War 1. This is the first group of African Americans trained as officers for the United States military.

1935 African Canadian Willie O'Ree is born in New Brunswick, Canada. O'Ree was the first Black professional hockey player.

1966 The Black Panther Party is formed by Huey Newton and Bobby Seale. The Black Panthers were established to rally African Americans to a common purpose of improving the economic and social conditions of Blacks.

2003 African American jazz trumpeter, and singer Louis Armstrong's home, a National Historic Landmark, is opened as a museum in New York City.

Tommie Smith Statue at the National Museum of African American History and Culture in Washington

 # OCTOBER 16

1833 African American teacher and diplomat, Ebenezer Don Carlos Bassett, is born in Litchfield, Connecticut. As United States minister to Haiti, Litchfield was the first African American diplomat.

. . . .

1859 White abolitionist John Brown and his small army of 21 attack Harpers Ferry, Virginia's Federal armory to encourage insurrection among the local slaves and other abolitionists. The attack failed and

Brown was hanged for his actions, but many believe these events were the spark that ignited the Civil War.

. . . .

1868 African American South Carolina State Senator, B. F. Randolph is assassinated in Abbeville. The crime was never solved.

. . . .

1932 Symphonic conductor and double bass player, Henry Lewis is born in Los Angeles, California. Lewis was the first African American

JAN
FEB
MAR
APR
MAY
JUN
JUL
AUG
SEP
OCT
NOV
DEC

to conduct a major symphony orchestra.

1968 African American Olympic athletes Tommie Smith and John Carlos are removed from the Mexico Olympic games for their raised, closed-fisted protest during the awards ceremony where Smith had won the gold medal and Carlos the bronze in the 200-meter race.

1995 The Million Man March occurs in Washington, D. C. The march was organized to promote a positive image of African American men and for legislators to acknowledge the issues of Black Americans.

 # OCTOBER 17

1817 Minister and African American abolitionist, Samuel Ward is born in Maryland. Ward was an active participant in the rescue of fugitive slaves.

1888 The Capital Savings Bank of Washington, D. C. opens. Capital Savings is one of the first banks opened for and operated by African Americans.

1924 The Phyllis Wheatley House in Minneapolis, Minnesota opens to provide social services in the predominately African American community of North Minneapolis.

1950 African American Actor, Howard Rollins, Jr. is born in Baltimore,

Maryland. Rollins most notable productions included the movie *Ragtime* and the television show "In the Heat of the Night."

1956 Mae Jemison, astronaut, doctor, and businesswoman is born in Decatur, Alabama. Jemison was the first Black woman in space.

1985 October 17 is established as Black Poetry Day in commemoration of the birth of Jupiter Hammon, the first published Black poet in the United States, and to celebrate the works of other influential Black poets.

2018 African American Marine Corps Sergeant Major John L. Canley is awarded the Medal of Honor for his conspicuous gallantry during the Viet Nam War.

 # OCTOBER 18

1758 The Old Bluff Church in Cumberland County, North Carolina is established. The Old Bluff Church was the site of the Battle of Averasboro during the Civil War.

1866 Dock Jordan, African American college professor and administrator, is born in South Carolina. Jordan was an advocate for the rights of Blacks in the South.

1896 Saint Agnes Hospital and Training School for Colored Nurses in Raleigh,

North Carolina opens. It was the only hospital to serve the African American community in the area.

1926 African American rock 'n roll innovator Chuck Berry is born in San Jose, California. He wrote and performed one of the most iconic rock and roll songs to date, "Johnny B. Goode."

1951 African American award-winning novelist Terry McMillan is born in Port Huron, Michigan. McMillian's novels include *Mama*, *Waiting to Exhale*, and *A Day Late and a Dollar Short*.

1956 African American architect and educator, Michaele Pride, is born in Granada Hillis, California. Pride was the first woman in California to open her own architecture firm.

1961 Wynton Marsalis, African American musician, and educator is born in New Orleans, Louisiana. Marsalis was the first person to win a Grammy Award in both classical and jazz categories in the same year.

 # OCTOBER 19

1858 Doctor and mayor, Alan Minns, is born in the Bahamas. Minns is elected mayor of Thetford, England, the first mayor in England of African descent.

JAN
FEB
MAR
APR
MAY
JUN
JUL
AUG
SEP
OCT
NOV
DEC

1922 Benjamin Scott, African American chemist, is born in Florence, South Carolina. Scott was a chemist on the Manhattan Project and the development of atomic weapons during WWII.

1923 Lawyer, civil rights advocate, and politician, Georgia Powers is born in Springfield. Kentucky. In 1967 Powers becomes the first African American woman elected to the Kentucky State Senate.

1923 Beatrix McCleary, psychiatrist, and children's advocate is born in Jacksonville, Florida. McCleary was Yale's first African American woman student.

1944 The U. S. Navy accepts the first African American women for service in Women Accepted for Volunteer Emergency Service (WAVES).

1944 Reggae musician, Peter Tosh is born in Jamaica. Tosh's collaboration with Bob Marley produced the reggae style of music.

1958 African American lawyer and television political analyst, Michael Steel is born at Andrews Air Force Base in Maryland.

  # OCTOBER 20

1849 William Washington Browne, teacher, minister, and entrepreneur is born in Habersham County, Georgia. Browne established the first African American owned and operated bank in the U. S.

1890 Ragtime and jazz pianist, Jelly Roll Morton, was born in New Orleans, Louisiana. Morton was an innovator in ragtime and jazz music arrangements.

1893 The first president of Kenya and founder of the Pan-African Federation, Jomo Kenyatta is born.

1914 Fayard Nicholas, African American dancer and choreographer, is born in Mobile, Alabama. Nicholas was known for his innovative tap-dancing routines with his brother, Harold.

1964 The first woman vice-president of the United States, Kamala Harris is born in Oakland, California.

1971 Calvin Broadus, Jr., African American rapper, and actor is born in Long Beach, California. Broadus is better known as Snoop Dog.

2006 The United States Air Force makes the history and accomplishments of the Tuskegee Airmen required curriculum for Air Force officers.

Snoop Dogg at BottleRock in Napa Valley in 2018

JAN
FEB
MAR
APR
MAY
JUN
JUL
AUG
SEP
OCT
NOV
DEC

OCTOBER 21

1844 Fredrick Douglass' third son, Charles Douglass, is born in Lynn, Massachusetts. Charles Douglass was the first African American to enlist in the Union Army during the Civil War.

1876 Daniel Holmes, African American minister, and social activist is born in Randolph County, Missouri. He was active in the integration of the University of Missouri-Columbia and the development of Lincoln High School in Kansas City for African American students.

1890 Lorenzo Turner, African American professor and linguist is born in Elizabeth City, North Carolina. He is best known for his study of the Gullah language and culture.

1917 African American band leader, and jazz trumpeter, Dizzy Gillespie, is born in Cheraw, South Carolina. Gillespie was an influential force in the development of jazz trumpet technique and bebop music.

1921 U. S. Naval nurse, Edit DeVoe, is born in Washington, D. C. Ms. DeVoe became the first African American nurse in the regular Navy.

1939 African American poet, and professor, Primus St. John, is born in New York, New York. St. John has written numerous collections of poetry and helped establish the Poets in the Schools Program, which is available across the nation.

1973 Alvin Bragg, politician, and lawyer is born in Harlem, New York. Bragg was elected as the first African American New York County District Attorney.

📑 OCTOBER 22

1800 African American Lewis Temple is born in Richmond, Virginia. Temple invented a whaling harpoon, "Temple's Toggle," that became the standard for whalers throughout the 1800s.

1830 Mary Dickerson, African American businesswoman and social club organizer is born in Haddam, Connecticut. Dickerson created the Women's Newport League, Northeastern Federation of Colored Women's Clubs, and the Rhode Island Union of Colored Women's Clubs.

1854 African American minstrel performer, and composer, James Bland, is born in Flushing, New York. Bland wrote over 700 songs and is known for composing the state song for Virginia, "Carry Me Back to Old Virginny."

1912 George (Leitao) Leighton, African American lawyer, judge, and civic activist was born in New Bedford, Maine. Leighton served as president of the NAACP, assistant

attorney general of Illinois, and elected as Cook County Court judge.

1917 African American lawyer, administrator, and diplomat, Franklin Williams, is born in Flushing, New York. Williams helped to organize the Peace Corps, was a representative to the United Nations, and served as ambassador to Ghana.

1936 Co-founder of the Black Panther Party, and social activist, Bobby Seale, was born in Dallas, Texas.

1941 African American historian, professor, and author, Rosalyn Terborg-Penn, is born in Brooklyn, New York. She was one of the first historians to document the contributions of African American women in the suffrage movement.

 # OCTOBER 23

1877 Natchez Seminary is established near Jackson, Mississippi. The United States Marine Hospital was purchased by the American Baptist Home Mission Society to create the school that eventually became Jackson State University. JSU is one

of the Historically Black Colleges and Universities.

1903 African American sports journalist and desegregationist, Sam Lacy is born in Washington, D. C. Lacey was a staunch supporter of an integrated National Baseball League and used his journalistic opportunities to promote desegregation in professional baseball.

1940 World-famous Afro Brazilian soccer player and philanthropist, Pelé, is born in Edson Arantes do Nascimento, Brazil. During his 29-year career, Pelé scored over 1250 goals.

1947 The National Association for the Advancement of Colored People (NAACP) presents a petition asking the United Nations to call the United States on their failings on human rights issues, especially in the causes of African Americans.

1958 African American minister, professor, and journalist, Michael Dyson is born. Dyson overcame his rough beginning as a gang member and teen father to earn his Ph. D. in Theology, become a national journalist, and Ivy-league professor.

OCTOBER 24

1896 African American cosmetologist, Marjorie Joyner, is born in Monterey, Virginia. Joyner created a hair wave machine that would curl hair, keeping the curl for many days.

1935 Langston Hughes' play *Mulatto: A Tragedy in the Deep South* opens on Broadway.

JAN
FEB
MAR
APR
MAY
JUN
JUL
AUG
SEP
OCT
NOV
DEC

JAN
FEB
MAR
APR
MAY
JUN
JUL
AUG
SEP
OCT
NOV
DEC

1948 Kweisi Mfume, African American politician, is born in Silver Spring, Maryland. Mfume has served as Baltimore City Councilman, Maryland Congressman and Senator, and president of the NAACP.

1964 Zambia achieves independence from Britain.

1978 *The Wiz*, a movie of the retelling of the *Wizard of Oz* with an all-Black cast opens in theaters. The movie featured Diana Ross and Michael Jackson.

1981 The National Coalition of 100 Black Women is founded. Originally established as the Coalition of 100 Black Women, it started with 24 women. It was instituted for promoting gender and racial equity. The NCBW currently has 60 chapters in 28 states.

 OCTOBER 25

1892 African American social activist, Irene McCoy Gaines, is born in Ocala, Florida. Gains was an administrator of the first branch of the Young Women's Christian Association (YWCA) in Chicago.

1901 Desegregationist and lawyer, Louis L. Redding is born in Alexandria, Virginia. Redding was the first African American lawyer in the state of Delaware. He also sued and won the case to integrate the University of Delaware.

1925 Member of the National Inventor's Hall of Fame and biochemist, African American Emmett Chappell, is born in Phoenix, Arizona.

1913 Professional golfer Bill Spiller is born in Tulsa, Oklahoma. Although Spiller was never able to play in the PGA, it was his efforts that integrated the Professional Golfers Association.

1947 African American writer and poet, Nathaniel Mackey, is born in Miami, Florida. Mackey has won multiple awards for his contemporary poetry.

1997 The Million Woman March took place in Philadelphia, Pennsylvania. The purpose was to bring attention to the issues facing African American women in American society.

2018 Ethiopia elects its first woman president, Sahle-Work Zewde.

 # OCTOBER 26

1899 Negro Leagues baseball player, and National Baseball Hall of Famer, William "Judy" Johnson, is born in Snow Hill, Maryland.

Johnson was the first African American to be an assistant coach in Major League Baseball.

JAN
FEB
MAR
APR
MAY
JUN
JUL
AUG
SEP
OCT
NOV
DEC

JAN
FEB
MAR
APR
MAY
JUN
JUL
AUG
SEP
OCT
NOV
DEC

1911 Considered one of the best gospel singers of all time, Mahalia Jackson, is born in New Orleans, Louisiana. Jackson was inducted into the Rock and Roll Hall of Fame in 1997.

1919 African American lawyer and politician, Edward Brooke, Jr., is born in Washington, D. C. He was the first African American to be elected by popular vote to the United States Senate from the state of Massachusetts.

1935 Highly regarded mathematician, Gloria Conyers Hewitt, is born in Sumpter, South Carolina. Hewitt was the first African American woman to chair a university math department in the U. S.

1938 Distinguished African American drummer, Jabo Starks, is born in Jackson, Alabama. Starks is known for playing with music greats James Brown and B. B. King.

1942 Afro Brazilian international singer and composer, Milton Nascimento, is born in Rio de Janeiro, Brazil. He is known for his collaborations with singing stars such as Earth, Wind, and Fire, Carlos Santana, and Paul Simon.

1956 Former United States Surgeon General, Regina Benjamin is born in Mobile, Alabama. Benjamin was the first African American woman elected to the board of the American Medical Association.

OCTOBER 27

1842 African American businessman, and community leader, Lewis Adams is born in Tuskegee, Alabama. Adams is credited with securing the promise for the Negro Normal School in Tuskegee, now Tuskegee University, from state Senator W. F. Foster.

1908 Notable African American photographer, Charles Harris, is born in Pittsburgh, Pennsylvania. He worked for the *Pittsburgh Courier*, a newspaper for African Americans, for almost 40 years.

1917 African American civil rights attorney, Anna Langford, is born in Springfield, Ohio.

Langford was the first woman elected to the Chicago City Council.

1922 Ruby Dee, African American actress and civil rights supporter is born in Cleveland, Ohio. Dee is known for the film *A Raisin in the Sun*, and the TV mini-series *Roots*.

1933 Baseball shortstop and second baseman, Pumpsie Green is born in Boley, Oklahoma. Green was the first African American to play for the Boston Red Sox.

1954 Benjamin O. Davis becomes the first African American promoted to Brigadier General in the United States Navy.

1979   Britain grants the island nation of Saint Vincent and the Grenadines its independence.

 ## OCTOBER 28

1798   Quaker abolitionist, Levi Coffin, is born in Guilford County, North Carolina. Coffin is credited with assisting over 2000 slaves along the Underground Railroad.

1861   Lawer and civil rights supporter, Federick McGhee, is born in Aberdeen, Mississippi. McGhee was the first African American lawyer in Minnesota. He was also one of the founders of the civil rights organization, the Niagara Movement.

1921   Arturo O'Farrill, Afro Cuban trumpet player, and big band composer and arranger is born in Havana, Cuba. O'Farrill was known for his jazz and Afro Cuban music.

1927   Black British singer, dancer, and actress, Cleo Lane is born in London, England. She won the 1986 Grammy Award for Best Female Jazz Vocal Performance.

1954   Carmen Jones one of the first mainstream movies with an all-African American cast opens in New York City.

1971   African American writer and publisher, Jessica Moore, is born in Detroit, Michigan. Moore has received

many recognitions for
her writings.
....

🗇 OCTOBER 29

1837 Harriet Powers, quilt artist, is born in Athens, Georgia. Powers was known for her Bible and Pictorial quilts, depicting Bible stories and other historical events, which are considered works of fine art.

....

1853 Civil rights advocate, teacher, and social organizer, Josephine Wilson Bruce, is born in Philadelphia. Bruce advocated for educational reforms for African American children, was a principal at the prestigious Tuskegee Institute, and organizer of several social groups for Black women.

....

1866 The Colored School of Watsonville, California is established when Robert Johnson petitions the Pajaro Valley School District for his children to be allowed to attend the public schools. The Colored School was closed in 1879 when segregation is abolished in the district.

....

1917 The Municipal Training School for Colored Nurses in Fulton County, Georgia is granted a charter.

....

1923 The show *Runnin' Wild* opens Broadway. The play included the dance "The Charleston" and the song of the same name, which both went on to become

JAN FEB MAR APR MAY JUN JUL AUG SEP OCT NOV DEC

international hits. The dance has its roots in African American dance.

1934 African American jazz saxophonist, Eddie Harris is born in Chicago, Illinois. Harris was famous for his

experimentation with instruments and sound.

1938 African politician Ellen Johnson Sirleaf is born in Monrovia, Liberia. Sirleaf was the president of Liberia from 2006-2018.

Ellen Johnson-Sirleaf speaks at the UN 72nd General Assembly in 2017

 OCTOBER 30

1860 William Edward White, baseball player and bookkeeper, was born in Milner, Georgia. White was the first African American to play professional baseball in the

National League. For reasons unknown he played only one game on June 21, 1937, for the Providence Grays.

1918 Frank M. Johnson, southern

American white lawyer, and Federal judge, is born in Haleyville, Alabama. Johnson's court rulings were critical in the fight against the Jim Crow laws of the south.

1922 African American inventor, Marie Van Brittan Brown, is born in Queens, New York. Brown invented the first home security and closed-circuit television surveillance system.

1930 Clifford Brown, African American jazz trumpeter, is born in Wilmington, Delaware. Brown was an influential trumpet player whose impact on the jazz world was greatly diminished by a fatal car crash in 1956.

1935 Mahmoud El-Kati, African American professor, and author, is born in Savannah, Georgia. El-Kati is known for his commentary and teachings on the African American experience and traditions.

1991 Black Entertainment Television (BET) becomes a publicly traded company.

 # OCTOBER 31

1896 African American singer and actress, Ethel Waters, is born in Chester, Pennsylvania. Waters was a popular and influential performer from the 1920s-1960s.

1848 Community leader and activist, Corvine Patterson,

is born in Roanoke, Missouri. Patterson was a prominent member in the African American community in Wyandotte, Kansas, a gathering place for newly freed slaves.

1905 Notorious gangster Ellsworth "Bumpy" Johnson is born in Charleston, South Carolina.

1905 African American Charles Patterson is granted a patent for improvements to the automobile dashboard.

1907 African American musician, arranger, and composer, Edgar Sampson is born in New York, New York. Sampson wrote or arranged many big band songs from the 1930s and 40s, his most notable being "Stompin' at the Savoy."

1947 Jennifer Hosten, model, flight attendant, and psychotherapist, is born in St. George's, Grenada. Hosten was the first Black woman to win the Miss World competition.

1950 Playing for the Washington Capitols, Earl Lloyd becomes the first African American to play in a National Basketball Association game.

1997 The support group Mocha Moms is formed with the goal of aiding and supporting work-at-home mothers of color.

NOVEMBER 1

1604 William Shakespeare's tragedy Othello is performed on this date at the Whitehall Palace in England. This stage classic is one of the first to feature a Black lead character.

1864 The 41st United States Colored Infantry is established. The Infantry was organized at Camp Penn in Philadelphia, Pennsylvania. Its members consisted of enlisted Black men that fought with the Union Army during the American Civil War.

1899 Aunt Jemima Pancake Mix begins selling in stores. It was the first ready-made pancake mix and became the most recognized brand in U.S. history. Quaker Oats has rebranded Aunt Jemima to make progress toward racial equality.

1910 W.E.B. Du Bois began publishing NAACP monthly magazine, *Crisis*.

1945 John H. Johnson publishes the 1st issue of *Ebony Magazine*, which sells 25,000 copies.

1963 Federal case, Simkins v. Moses H. Cone Hospital, is decided that separate but equal racial segregation in publicly funded hospitals violates equal protection under the United States Constitution.

JAN
FEB
MAR
APR
MAY
JUN
JUL
AUG
SEP
OCT
NOV
DEC

NOVEMBER 2

1787 The African Free School in New York City opens. It is the first school for Blacks in America.

1875 The Mississippi Plan goes into effect. The plan was devised by white conservatives to interfere with Black political participation through intimidation.

1884 The Philadelphia Tribune is established in Philadelphia, Pennsylvania. It is the longest continuously published African American newspaper in the United States.

1900 The American Negro Exhibit is shown at the World's Fair Exposition in Paris, France. The exhibit highlights the progress of African American lives at the turn of the century.

1903 Maggie Walker opens St. Lukes Penny Savings Bank in Richmond, Virginia. It is the first bank owned by a Black woman in America.

1974 Cornell Haynes, Jr., known as the rapper Nelly, is born in Austin, Texas.

1983 Martin Luther King Day Bill is signed. The official holiday begins on the 3rd Monday of January 1986.

JAN
FEB
MAR
APR
MAY
JUN
JUL
AUG
SEP
OCT
 NOV
DEC

NOVEMBER 3

1868 John W. Menard makes history as the first Black person elected to the United States Congress.

1882 John Baxter Taylor, the 1st African American Olympic Gold Medalist, is born in Washington, D. C. He was awarded the gold medal for the track and field medley relay in the 1908 Olympics.

1929 The All Negro Hour premieres on American radio. It was the first radio program to exclusively features all Black artists.

1957 The Manifesto on Racial Beliefs is published in the Atlanta Constitution newspaper. The manifesto, signed by 79 white clergymen in the South, condemned the hatred and violence which followed the ruling from Supreme Court on Brown v. Board of Education.

1964 A.W. Willis Jr. makes history as first Black person elected to the General Assembly in Tennessee since Reconstruction.

1992 Carol Mosely Braun, is the first African American woman elected to the United States Senate.

JAN
FEB
MAR
APR
MAY
JUN
JUL
AUG
SEP
OCT
NOV
DEC

NOVEMBER 4

1920 Eileen Jackson Southern, musicologist, was born in Minneapolis, Minnesota. Ms. Jackson is the first Black woman to be a full tenured professor at Harvard University.

1922 The burial place of Black Egyptian King Tut is discovered. The find by Howard Carter and Lord Carnarvon is noted because the tomb was untouched by thieves.

1969 Entertainment mogul Sean "Diddy" Combs (Puff Daddy) is born in Harlem, New York.

1981 Zina Garrison is the first Black player to win the junior singles tennis championship at Wimbledon.

2008 Barack Obama becomes the 44th President of the United States. He is the first African American to be elected to the position.

2014 Mia Love is the first Black Republican woman to be elected to congress in U. S. history. She was voted to represent the state of Utah.

NOVEMBER 5

1836 Theo Wright is the first African American to receive a theological degree in the United States.

1887 Rene Maran, Afro Caribbean French journalist is the first Black writer to win the prestigious French literary prize, the Prix Goncourt.

1899, James Banning, aviator, is born in Oklahoma. He was the first Black aviator to receive a license from the US. Department of Commerce.

1901 Etta Moten Barnett, stage singer and actress, is born in Weimar, Texas. Ms. Barnett is famous for her Broadway performances of Sugar Hill, Lysistrata, and Porgy and Bess. Molten was the 2nd Black stage artist to perform at the White House.

1917 The Supreme Court ruled on the case Buchanan v. Warley. William Warley a Black buyer made an offer to Charles Buchanan for property in a white neighborhood. The court ruled that separation of races was inappropriate and unconstitutional.

1974 Walter E. Washington becomes first elected African American mayor of Washington, D.C. He is first Black mayor of any major U. S. city.

 # NOVEMBER 6

1880 George Poage, African American Olympian, and teacher is born in Hannibal, Missouri. He took the bronze medals for finishing 3rd in the 200- and 400-meter hurdles in the 1904 Olympics.

JAN
FEB
MAR
APR
MAY
JUN
JUL
AUG
SEP
OCT
NOV
DEC

1901 Juanita Hall, singer, and actress, is born in Keyport, NJ. Ms. Hall is recognized for her performances as Julie in *Show Boat*, and Bloody Mary in the Broadway and film adaptations of *South Pacific*.

1920 W.E.B. Du Bois is awarded the Spingarn medal by the NAACP. He is awarded the medal for his work on the organization of the Pan African Congress.

1973 Coleman A. Young is elected the first African American mayor of Detroit.

1990 Sharon Pratt was elected as the first African American woman Mayor of Washington D.C.

First Lady Hillary Clinton gets a hug and a kiss from DC Mayor Sharon Pratt Kelly

 # NOVEMBER 7

1934 Arthur L. Mitchell defeats Oscar DePriest in Chicago to become the first Black Democratic congressman.

1950 The first African American woman neurosurgeon, Alexa Canady, is born in Lancing, Michigan.

1955 The Supreme Court rules that public golf courses must be integrated in Holmes v. Atlanta.

1963 Elston Howard becomes the first African American to receive the National Baseball's American League's Most Valuable Player award.

1972 Barbara Jordan and Andrew Young are the first African Americans to be elected to Congress in the South since reconstruction.

1989 David Dinkins makes history as first Black mayor of New York City.

1991 The legendary musician Jimi Hendrix is inducted into the Rock and Roll Hall of Fame.

NOVEMBER 8

1919 Black Canadian National Hockey League player, Herbert Carnegie, is born in Toronto, Canada. Carnegie has been inducted into both the Canada and Ontario Sports Halls of Fame.

1947 African American singer, Minnie Riperton, is born in Chicago, Illinois. With the widest vocal range of any singer in her generation, her most famous song is "Lovin' You."

JAN
FEB
MAR
APR
MAY
JUN
JUL
AUG
SEP
OCT
NOV
DEC

JAN
FEB
MAR
APR
MAY
JUN
JUL
AUG
SEP
OCT

NOV
DEC

1965 The first bill to address discrimination in the United Kingdom, the Race Relations Act of 1965, is passed by Parliament.

1966 Edward W. Brooke from Massachusetts is elected as the first African American Senator since Reconstruction.

1970 Kevin Young, poet and director of the National Museum of African American History and Culture, is born in Lincoln, Nebraska. Young has received many awards and accolades for his poetry.

2006 The first elected Muslim Congressman, Keith Ellison, is voted into office in Minneapolis, Minnesota.

2006 The state of Massachusetts elects Deval Patrick as its first African American Governor.

 # NOVEMBER 9

1731 African American scientist and inventor Benjamin Banneker is born free in Ellicott, Maryland. Banneker's accomplishments included working on the design of Washington, D. C. and publishing an annual almanac.

1815 African American minister and abolitionist Leonard Grimes is born in Leesburg, Virginia. As a conductor on the Underground Railroad, Grimes helped deliver many enslaved Blacks to freedom.

1935 Robert Gibson, African American Baseball Hall of Famer, is born in Omaha, Nebraska. Gibson pitched for the St. Louis Cardinals from 1959-1975.

1956 Mattiwilda Dobbs makes history as the first Black person to sing as a romantic lead at the New York Metropolitan Opera.

1975 Singer Sisqo of the rap group Dru Hill is born in Baltimore, Maryland.

1999 The "Little Rock Nine" receive the Congressional Medal of Honor for their courage and determination in the face of discrimination.

 # ПОVEMBER 10

1735 Granville Sharpe, a white British abolitionist, is born in Durham, England. Sharpe worked closely with Wilber Wilberforce and Thomas Clarkson to eliminate the slave trade in England.

1898 The Wilmington Massacre occurs as mobs of white men protest the city's elected Black officials. It is estimated that up to 300 African Americans were murdered at the time.

1930 The first African American Chairman of the Civil Rights commission, Clarence Pendleton, Jr. is born in Louisville, Kentucky.

1956 Actor and comedian, David Adkins, is born in Benton Harbor, Michigan. Adkins is better known as Sinbad.

1957 Charlie Sifford becomes the first African American to win a Professional Golfer's Association tournament at the Long Beach Open in California.

1960 Andrew T. Hatcher named associate press secretary by President John F. Kennedy, making history as the first Black person to hold the position.

 ## NOVEMBER 11

1782 White abolitionist Elihu Embree is born in Pennsylvania. Embree was the publisher of the first newspaper in the United States to promote the antislavery cause, The Manumission Intelligencier.

1890 Black inventor Charles Damiel McCree receives a patent for his portable fire escape.

1895 African American sculptor, Beulah Ecton Woodard, is born in Frankfort, Ohio. Woodard helped to organize the Los Angeles Negro Art Association.

1907 Playwright, teacher, and social activist, Shirley Graham DuBois, is born in Evansville, Indiana. W.E.B. DuBois was her second husband.

1914 Daisy Gatson Bates, president of the NAACP in Arkansas in 1952, was born in Huttig, Arkansas. Bates was instrumental in integrating Central High School in Little Rock.

1929 Lavern Baker, African American pop, and R&B singer from the 1950s and 60s, is born in Chicago, Illinois. Baker has been entered into both the Rock and Roll, and National Rhythm and Blues Halls of Fame.

1975 Angola becomes an independent nation when the ruling Portuguese are forced to leave the country due to civil war.

1978 Industrial engineer Paula Marcela Moreno Zapata is born in Bogota, Colombia. Zapata was the youngest and first Afro Colombian to hold the position of Minister of Culture of Colombia.

🗐 NOVEMBER 12

1815 White abolitionist and suffragist, Elizabeth Cady Stanton, is born in Johnstown, New York. Stanton is credited with being one of the founders of the Women's Rights Movement.

1863 William Edmondson, sculptor, is born in Davidson County, Tennessee. His exhibition at the New York Museum

JAN FEB MAR APR MAY JUN JUL AUG SEP OCT NOV DEC

of Modern Art made him the first African American to have a solo exhibition in the United States.

1876 Black comedian and entertainer, Bert Williams is born in New Providence, Bahamas. Williams partnered with George Walker to bring several plays with an all-Black cast to Broadway.

1906 African American Booker T. Washington White, pioneering Delta blues guitarist, is born in Houston, Mississippi. "Bukka" White was inducted into the Blues Hall of Fame in 1990.

1941 The National Negro Opera Company is established in Pittsburgh, Pennsylvania by Mary Cardwell Dawson.

 # NOVEMBER 13

1894 African American inventor Albert Richardson receives a patent for his casket lowering device.

1911 The first African American major league baseball coach, Buck O'Neil is born in Carrabelle, Florida.

1920 Graphic designer, George Olden, is born in Birmingham, Alabama. Olden was the first African American to design a United States postage stamp.

1940 The Supreme Court rules that African Americans cannot be prevented from purchasing homes in white neighborhoods in Hansberry v. Lee.

1949 Born Caryn Elaine Johnson, African American actress and television personality, Whoopi Goldberg, is born in Manhattan, New York. Goldberg was the first African American woman to win an Emmy, a Grammy, an Oscar, and a Tony Award.

2006 Ground is broken for the Martin Luther King, Jr. National Memorial in Washington, D. C. The memorial was completed and dedicated on August 28, 2011.

NOVEMBER 14

1832 African American nun, and teacher, Mathilda Beasley is born in New Orleans, Louisiana. Beasley opened the first orphanage in Georgia for Black girls.

1915 Figure skating pioneer, and coach Mabel Fairbanks is born in Florida. Although Fairbanks was never allowed to compete because of her race, she opened doors for others of color to participate in ice skating competitions.

1917 Doris Hollis Pemberton, reporter, and education advocate, is born in Nacogdoches, Texas. Pemberton was the first African American to cover the Democratic Convention in Texas.

JAN FEB MAR APR MAY JUN JUL AUG SEP OCT NOV DEC

1934 Patriarch of the musical Marsalis family dynasty, Ellis Marsalis, Jr., is born in New Orleans, Louisiana. Marsalis was a globally-respected African American jazz pianist and music teacher.

1950 African American Lydia Holmes receives a patent for wooden pull-toy.

1954 Condoleezza Rice, politician, and international policy maker is born in Birmingham, Alabama. Rice was the first African American woman to hold the post of United States Secretary of State.

1960 The Supreme Court rules in Gomillion v. Lightfoot that it is illegal to draw electoral boundaries to benefit a political party or candidate.

1969 Diversity Information Resources becomes an incorporated business. DIR works to help businesses develop a broad diversity of employees and business partnerships.

Secretary of State Condoleezza Rice at a press conference in Berlin in 2007

NOVEMBER 15

1850 Emanuel Hewlett, African American lawyer, judge, and civil rights advocate is born in Brooklyn, New York. Hewlett aggressively fought for equal access to public houses for himself and other African Americans.

1866 The Pilgrim Baptist Church holds its inaugural service in St. Paul, Minnesota. The church was established by a group of escaped slaves and the first Black Baptist church in St. Paul.

1884 The Berlin Conference was begun to allow European interests to split the territories of Africa for European colonization.

1884 The Freedmen's Hospital Training School for Nurses is established in Washington, D. C.

1890 James Morris, Sr., lawyer, and newspaper publisher is born in Atlanta, Georgia. Morris helped to establish the Negro Bar Association.

1898 African American Lyda Newman receives a patent for a hairbrush with detachable bristles.

1950 Arthur Dorrington becomes the first Black man to sign with a professional hockey team, the New York Rangers.

NOVEMBER 16

1862 Ida Gibbs, Black teacher, suffragist, and social activist is born in Victoria, British Columbia, Canada. Gibbs was in the first class to graduate from Oberlin College in Ohio.

1863 Oakwood Industrial School, a Seventh-day Adventist, and United Negro College Fund institution, is opened in Huntsville, Alabama. It has been known as Oakwood University as of 2008 and is a HBCU.

1901 African American song writer and performer, Jesse Stone is born in Atchison, Kansas. Stone wrote the iconic Rock and Roll songs, "Rock Around the Clock," and "Shake Rattle and Roll."

1920 The first African American elected judge in Louisiana since the Reconstruction, Israel Meyer Augustine, Jr., is born in New Orleans.

1946 Joseph "Jo Jo" Henry White, African American basketball star of the 1970s, is born in St. Louis, Missouri. White received a gold medal in the 1968 Olympics as a member of the American Olympic basketball team.

1963 Professional tennis player and civic leader, Zina Garrison, is born in Houston, Texas. Garrison won a gold medal in the 1988 Olympics in doubles tennis.

1967 Actress and model, Lisa Bonet, is

born in San Francisco, California. Bonet is most recognizable from her role as Denise on the Cosby Show.

NOVEMBER 17

1809   Stephen Foster, white abolitionist, is born in Canterbury, New Hampshire. Foster was a passionate speaker and supporter of the anti-slavery movement.

1904   Lawyer, judge, and governor, William Hastie, is born in Knoxville, Tennessee. Hastie was the first African American to be appointed to the position of Territorial Governor of the U. S. Virgin Islands.

1911   The Black fraternity Omega Psi Phi is established by Edgar Love, Oscar Cooper, and Frank Coleman. The core beliefs of the fraternity are manhood, scholarship, perseverance, and up-lift.

1969   African American feminist, Alice Walker, is born in Jackson, Mississippi. Walker is a globally recognized voice on third-wave feminism.

NOVEMBER 18

1899   Howard Thurman, human rights activist, and advocate for peaceful protest, was born in Daytona Beach, Florida.

JAN
FEB
MAR
APR
MAY
JUN
JUL
AUG
SEP
OCT
NOV
DEC

Thurman was the first African American dean of Marsh Chapel at Boston University.

1917 Professor and physicist Carolyn Parker is born in Gainesville, Florida. Parker is the first African American to receive a master's degree in physics.

1936 Internationally known jazz trumpeter Don Cherry is born in Oklahoma City, Oklahoma. Cherry was revolutionary in the style of fusion jazz.

1952 Black British American stage, and screen actor, Delroy Lindo is born in Lewisham, London, England. Lindo has received many awards including a NAACP Image Award in 2009.

1956 Warren Moon, African American professional football quarterback, is born in Los Angeles, California. Moon has the exclusive honor of being the only player to belong to both the National Football Hall of Fame and the Canadian Football Hall of Fame.

1968 African American major league baseball player, Gary Sheffield is born in Tampa, Florida. Sheffield is the only baseball player to play in All Stars game for 5 different teams.

 # NOVEMBER 19

1845 Author, social activist, and teacher, Frances Ann Rollin Whipper, is born in

Charleston, South Carolina. Whipper wrote *The Life and Public Services of Martin R. Delany.* It was the first full-length biography by an African American.

. . . .

1875 The first woman to teach at an accredited law school, African American Lutie Lytle, is born in Murfreesboro, Tennessee.

. . . .

1911 William Attaway, African American playwright, actor, novelist, and song writer is born in Greenville, Mississippi. Attaway was the first African American script writer for TV and movies. His most notable writing was the song "Day-o Banana Boat Song" for Harry Belafonte.

. . . .

1915 The acting company the Lafayette

Players opens their first show in Harlem. The Lafayette Players were a stock group of African American actors focused on dramatic acting, as opposed to comedy, and singing roles.

. . . .

1921 One of baseball's all-time greatest catchers, Roy Campanella, is born in Philadelphia, Pennsylvania. Campanella played in 5 World Series in his nine-year baseball career.

. . . .

1973 African American master tap dancer and choreographer Savion Glover is born in Newark, New Jersey. Glover is responsible for the choreography and dancing in the animated movie *Happy Feet.*

. . . .

JAN
FEB
MAR
APR
MAY
JUN
JUL
AUG
SEP
OCT
NOV
DEC

JAN
FEB
MAR
APR
MAY
JUN
JUL
AUG
SEP
OCT

NOV
DEC

Savion Glover performs at the Jazz Foundation of America benefit concert in 2019

 # NOVEMBER 20

1827 Prolific composer, conductor, and musician, Edmond Dédé, is born in New Orlean, Louisiana.

1865 Sayne School, later to become Talladega College, is established in Talladega, Alabama. Talladega College is an HBUC.

1879 Charles Gilpin, actor, and singer is born in Richmond, Virginia. In 1920 Gilpin was the first African American to be recognized by the Drama League of New York as one of the 10 most influential people in theater.

1910 The first African American Deputy Attorney General for California, Anna Pauli Murray is born in Baltimore, Maryland.

1923 African American Garrett Morgan receives a patent for his traffic signal.

1960 The country of Brazil institutes Black Awareness Day.

1976 Olympic gymnast, Dominique Dawes, is born in Silver Spring, Maryland. Dawes was the first woman of African descent to receive an Olympic gold medal in gymnastics.

🗐 NOVEMBER 21

1842 The Sisters of the Holy Family congregation is founded in New Orleans, Louisiana to teach slaves, and care for the poor and elderly, they were the first African American order in the American South.

1882 The founder of the Piney Woods Country Life School, African American Laurence Jones, is born in St. Joseph, Missouri.

1931 The first annual meeting of the Association of Southern Women for the Prevention of Lynching is held in Atlanta, Georgia. This organization of influential white women was dedicated to stop lynchings in the South.

1933 Etta Zuber Falconer, African American mathematician, professor, and mentor, is born in Tupelo, Mississippi.

1936 Master orchestra conductor James DePreist is born in Philadelphia, Pennsylvania.

JAN FEB MAR APR MAY JUN JUL AUG SEP OCT NOV DEC

1962 Professional bowler, George Branham, III, is born in Detroit, Michigan. Branham was the first African American to win the bowling Tournament of Champions.

1969 Baseball Hall of Famer, Ken Griffey Jr. is born in Donora, Pennsylvania. Griffey won 10 Golden Glove awards and hit over 600 homeruns during his career.

 ## NOVEMBER 22

1908 Engineer, pilot, and military instructor, Fank Mann is born in Houston, Texas. Mann was an aviation instructor for the Tuskegee Airmen, and the first African American pilot for American Airways.

1916 William Powell, the first African American to design, build, and own a golf course, is born in Greenville, Alabama.

1919 John Holloman, Jr., African American doctor, U. S. Army Captain, and civil rights advocate, is born in Washington, D. C.

1922 Kenneth O. Wofford, Sr., Tuskegee Airman, and U. S. Air Force Colonel is born in Wagoner, Oklahoma. Wofford has been awarded numerous military and civilian commendations.

1942 Guion "Guy" Bluford, the first African American in space, is born

JAN
FEB
MAR
APR
MAY
JUN
JUL
AUG
SEP
OCT

NOV
DEC

in Philadelphia, Pennsylvania.

1952 Ambassador to the United Nations, Ambassador to Liberia, and diplomat, Linda Thomas-Greenfield

is born in Baker, Louisiana.

1989 Colonel Frederick D. Gregory makes history as the first African American to lead a space mission.

 # NOVEMBER 23

1805 Jamaican nurse and caregiver, Mary Grant Seacole, is born in Kingston, Jamaica. With her own funding Seacole went to the Crimean front in 1855 to nurse wounded soldiers.

1863 African American lawyer, politician, and civil rights advocate, Warner McGuinn, is born in Goochland, Virginia.

1939 Betty Everett, pop and R&B singer,

is born in Greenwood, Mississippi. Everett's most popular song is "The Shoop Shoop Song."

1946 Civil Rights Activist and Illinois Congressman Bobby Lee Rush is born in Albany, Georgia. He served as the Congressman from the Illinois first district from 1993-2023.

1955 Harolyn Blackwell, accomplished operatic and Broadway

JAN
FEB
MAR
APR
MAY
JUN
JUL
AUG
SEP
OCT
NOV
DEC

soprano, was born in Washington, D. C.

. . . .

1960 African American television broadcaster Robin Roberts is born in Tuskegee, Alabama.

. . . .

1990 August Wilson's African American drama, *The Piano Lesson,* wins the Pulitzer Prize for drama.

. . . .

 # NOVEMBER 24

1866 Rust College in Holly Springs, Mississippi, is established with the cooperation of Freedman's Aid Society and the Methodist Episcopal Church. Rust is an HBCU.

1868 Master ragtime pianist, African American Scott Joplin, is born in Texarkana, Texas. As a pioneer in ragtime piano, Joplin's most famous works include "Original Rags," "Maple Leaf Rag," and "The Entertainer."

. . . .

1912 African American swing pianist, Teddy Wilson is born in Austin, Texas. Wilson played with such music luminaries as Benny Goodman, Billie Holiday, and Louis Armstrong.

. . . .

1914 Bessie Blout, inventor, physical therapist, and forensic scientist is born in Hickory, Virginia. Blout was the first Black woman to train and work at Scottland Yard in England.

. . . .

1920 Tuskegee Airman, lawyer and civil rights advocate, Percy Sutton, is born in San Antonio, Texas. At the time, Sutton was the highest ranking African American elected official in New York City.

1974 The fossilized bones of "Lucy" are discovered in Ethiopia.

2017 Zimbabwe elects Emmerson Mnangagwa as president.

 # NOVEMBER 25

1879 Simmons College is established in Louisville, Kentucky. Simmons is one of the Historically Black Colleges and Universities in the United States.

1903 Olympic track and field athlete, William Hubbard, is born in Cincinnati, Ohio. Competing in the long jump event at the 1924 Olympics he became the first Black athlete to win an individual Olympic gold medal.

1946 African American owned Broadway Federal Bank in California receives its charter for business.

1949 Ralph J. Bunche awarded Spingarn Medal from the National Association for the Advancement of Colored People for his achievements as UN mediator of the Palestine conflict in 1949.

1949 Ace African American tap dancer

Bill "Bojangles" Robinson passes away. Robinson was the first African American dancer to appear in a film with a white partner, Shirley Temple, in *The Little Colonel*.

1953 African American master photographer, Dawoud Bey, is born in New York, New York. Bey's photographs have been exhibited throughout the United States.

1975 The African country of Suriname gains independence.

2009 Ozzie Newsome becomes the first African American to head a National Football League team, when he is hired by the Baltimore Ravens to be the General Manager.

NOVEMBER 26

1858 Katherine Drexel, white Catholic nun, is born in Philadelphia, Pennsylvania. Drexel, a wealthy heiress, established the Sisters of the Blessed Sacrament, to provide support and educational opportunities for African Americans and Native Americans.

1878 Marshall Taylor, epic cyclist, was born in Indianapolis, Indiana. Taylor was the first African American to win a world cycling title.

1879 Personal librarian to J. P. Morgan, Belle Da Costa Green, is born in Washington, D. C. Greene was the first African American elected to the distinguished intellectual group Medieval Academy of America.

. . . .

1905 John Robinson, pilot, and equal rights activist is born in Carrabelle, Florida. Robinson was the first African American to attend the prominent Curtiss-Wright School of Aviation and initiated the pilots' program at the Tuskegee Institute.

. . . .

1933 William Lucy, union leader and engineer, is born in Memphis, Tennessee. Lucy was one of the organizers of the Coalition of Black Trade Unionists.

. . . .

1939 International singing sensation Anna Mae Bullock is born in Brownsville, Tennessee. Adopting the name Tina Turner, she became one of the most recognizable and honored singers in history. Her theme song became the iconic "Proud Mary."

. . . .

1969 Internationally known artist, Kara Walker, is born in Stockton, California. Walker is known for her unique silhouette-based artwork.

. . . .

Tina Turner's star on the Hollywood Walk of Fame

JAN
FEB
MAR
APR
MAY
JUN
JUL
AUG
SEP
OCT
NOV
DEC

NOVEMBER 27

1857 Robert Terrell, respected judge, lawyer, and professor is born in Orange, Virginia.

1870 African American teacher and philanthropist, Carrie Thomas Jordan, is born in Jacksonville, Florida.

1884 The Philadelphia Tribune is established in Philadelphia, Pennsylvania. It is the longest continuously published African American newspaper in the United States.

1923 African American mathematical child prodigy, J. Ernest Wilkins, Jr. is born in Chicago, Illinois. Wilkins received his B. S. degree at the age of 17 and his doctorate at the age of 19.

1942 Pioneering African American rock guitarist, Jimi Hendrix, is born in Seattle, Washington. Rolling Stone Magazine named Hendrix the greatest guitar player of all time.

1964 African American actress and model Robin Givens is born in New York City.

1976 Jaleel White, child actor is born in Culver City, California. His most prominent role was as Steve Urkel on the comedy series *Family Matters*.

JAN
FEB
MAR
APR
MAY
JUN
JUL
AUG
SEP
OCT
NOV
DEC

NOVEMBER 28

1868 William H. Lewis, football player, lawyer, and civil rights advocate, is born in Berkley, Virginia. He was the first African American to be named an All-American football player.

1907 Master artist, teacher, and administrator, Charles Alston, is born in Charlotte, North Carolina. His best-known work of art is a bust of Martin Luther King, Jr. for the White House.

1914 African American Owen Dodson, professor, writer, and playwright is born in Brooklyn, New York.

1914 Gertrude Hadley Jeannette, African American actress, playwright, and director is born in Urbana, Arkansas.

1929 Song writer, music producer, and Motown founder Berry Gordy, Jr. is born in Detroit, Michigan. Gordy developed Motown into the biggest African American financial business of its day.

 # NOVEMBER 29

1888 The first African American to hold the position of assistant attorney general for the state of Illinois, Nathan McGill,

lawyer, and publisher, was born in Quincy, Florida.

1907 Editor and journalist, Thomas Flemings, is born in Jacksonville, Florida. Flemings was the longest running journalist in a Black newspaper, contributing to the Sun-Reporter for over 50 years.

1915 African American pianist, and composer, Billy Strayhorn is born in Dayton, Ohio. "Take the A Train" performed by Duke Ellington's band is probably his most enduring composition.

1940 Thelma Mothershed, one of the "Little Rock Nine" is born in Bloomberg, Texas.

1958 Maria Moyano Delgado, Afro Peruvian activist, is born in Lima, Peru. Delgado worked to support soup kitchens and Vaso de Leche (Glass of Milk) to provide a daily glass of milk to the poor children of Lima.

1976 Chadwick Boseman, African American actor, is born in Anderson, South Carolina. Boseman was a popular actor in such films as Marvel's *Black Panther*, and 42, in which he portrayed the iconic baseball player Jackie Robinson.

1984 African American musical artist, Prince, performs a free surprise at Gallaudet University, school for the deaf.

2021 Singer Rihanna named National Hero of Barbados.

NOVEMBER 30

1835 White writer, lecturer, and abolitionist, Mark Twain, is born in Florida, Missouri.

1912 Photojournalist, and moviemaker, Gordon Parks is born in Fort Scott, Kansas. Parks was the first African American to write, produce, and direct a major Hollywood movie, *The Learning Tree* (1969).

1919 African American doctor, and medical researcher, Jane Cooke Wright, is born in New York City.

1924 Shirley Chisholm, the first United States African American woman congressional representative, is born in New York, New York.

1953 June Pointer, of the African American singing group The Pointer Sisters, is born in Oakland, California. She sang the lead vocals for the popular songs "He's So Shy," and "Jump (for My Love)."

1953 Michael Espy, lawyer, and congressman, is born in Yazoo City, Mississippi. Espy was the first African American Congressman from Mississippi since Reconstruction.

1966 The country of Barbados receives independence from Great Britain.

JAN
FEB
MAR
APR
MAY
JUN
JUL
AUG
SEP
OCT
NOV
DEC

1865 Shaw University is founded in Raleigh, North Carolina. It was the first of the Historically Black Colleges and Universities established in the South.

1874 The oldest African American women's sorority, the Order of the Eastern Star, is established in Washington, D. C.

1876 Blanche Wilkins Williams, teacher, and disability advocate, is born in La Corsse, Wisconsin. Ms. William is the first deaf Black woman to graduate from the Minnesota School for the Deaf in 1893.

1905 W.E.B. Du Bois publishes the first issue of his short-lived The Moon Illustrated Weekly magazine. It was the first nationally published illustrated magazine for African Americans.

1925 James Ford, educator, politician, and activist is born in Leon County, Florida. Ford was the first African American to become the mayor of any state capitol city.

1933 Three-time Grammy Award winning singer Louis Allen Rawls is born in Chicago, Illinois. His biggest song being "You'll Never Find Another Love Like Mine."

1955 Rosa Parks is arrested in Montgomery, Alabama for refusing to give

JAN
FEB
MAR
APR
MAY
JUN
JUL
AUG
SEP
OCT
NOV
DEC

up her seat in the whites only section of the public bus. This incident set the stage for the Montgomery Bus Boycott and became the turning point in the Civil Rights struggle.

1940 African American comedian, and actor Richard Franklin Lennox Pryor III is born in Peoria, Illinois. Pryor's comedy was famous for dealing with controversial topics and the Black experience. He influenced generations of performers as a stand-up comedian and comedic actor.

Sculpture of Rosa Parks at the National Civil Rights Museum

 # DECEMBER 2

1863 Phillip Reed, Black slave, places the Freedom statue on top of the White House dome. Reed worked at Bladensburg Foundry in Maryland and supervised the casting of the bronze statue.

1874 Carlos Posadas, Afro-Argentinean

JAN
FEB
MAR
APR
MAY
JUN
JUL
AUG
SEP
OCT
NOV
DEC

composer, and musician is born in Buenos Aires, Argentina. The influence of Posada's compositions can still be heard in the modern tango of today.

1891 African American historian, teacher, and minister Charles H. Wesley is born in Louisville, Kentucky. Wesley was one of the first proponents of African American studies.

1903 Teacher, and government administrator, Alfred E. Smith, is born in Hot Springs, Arkansas. Smith was a member of Pres. Franklin Roosevelts "Black Cabinet."

1919 Norma Miller, dancer, and choreographer is born in Harlem, New York. Ms. Miller traveled the world through dance and eventually produced and starred in shows.

1928 Evelyn Fairbanks, writer, is born in Saint Paul, Minnesota. Ms. Fairbanks is most famous for her book "The Days of Rondo," a memoir of growing up in the 30's and 40's in the community of Rondo in Saint Paul.

1969 Marie V. Brittan Brown granted patent for first-of-its-kind closed-circuit home security system.

1975 African American Ohio State football player Archie Griffin makes history as the only athlete ever to win the Heisman Trophy twice.

DECEMBER 3

1847 The anti-slavery North Star newspaper is published by Frederick Douglas. The newspaper adopts the motto, "Right is of no sex, Truth is of no color, God is the Father of us all and we are all brethren."

1855 John Wesley Edward Bowen, teacher, and minister is born in New Orleans, Louisiana. Bowen was a member of the first graduating class of New Orleans University, one of the Historically Black Colleges and Universities.

1882 Ellis Ruley, African American folk artist, is born in Norwich, Connecticut. Ruley is known for his primitive and unique technique in subjects that are generally peaceful and calming.

1911 University professor and government administrator, Helen Edmonds is born in Lawrenceville, Virginia. She was appointed special emissary to Liberia by Pres. Eisenhower.

1922 African American chemist, professor, and researcher, Ralph Gardner, is born in Cleveland, Ohio. Gardner has the distinction of working on the Manhattan Project during World War II.

1941 African American psychologist, sociologist, and author,

JAN
FEB
MAR
APR
MAY
JUN
JUL
AUG
SEP
OCT
NOV

Terrence Roberts is born in Little Rock, Arkansas. Roberts was one of the first students, known as the Little Rock Nine, to integrate into Little Rock's Central High School.

1951 African American nurse and midwife, Maude E. Callen, is celebrated in *Life Magazine* for her help, compassion, and comfort as she ministered to countless patients in Pineville, South Carolina.

 # DECEMBER 4

1906 Alpha Phi Alpha Fraternity is the first intercollegiate Greek letter fraternity for African American men. It was founded by seven Black men at Cornell University in Ithaca, New York who felt the need for a brotherhood among African descendants.

1923 The Cotton Club in New York City opens. The Cotton Club is a popular segregated night club with a cast of many of the most important Black performers and exclusively White clientele.

1942 The Burma Road project begins construction. This was WW II three-year military excavation project to re-open the Burma Road which India and China. The majority of the project's workers were Black soldiers.

DECEMBER 5

1870 William (Bill) Pickett, African Cherokee Cowboy, is born in Williamson County, Texas. He was inducted into the Pro-Rodeo Hall of Fame and the National Cowboy Hall of Fame in Oklahoma City.

1870 Benedict School and Institute, eventually Benedict College, opens in Columbia, South Carolina. Benedict College is one of the Historically Black Colleges and Universities.

1874 John Shippen Jr., African American golfer, is born in Washington D.C. At the age of 16 he was encouraged to enter the 2nd U.S. Open. He placed 5th in the event.

1899 Modjeska Simkins, social and health reformer, and civil rights activist, is born in Columbia, South Carolina. As the director of Negro Work for the South Carolina Tuberculosis Association, she was the state's only full-time Black public health worker in 1931.

1935 Mary McLeod Bethune establishes The National Council of Negro Women to unite women and promote the improvement of life for women and their families.

JAN
FEB
MAR
APR
MAY
JUN
JUL
AUG
SEP
OCT
NOV
DEC

DECEMBER 6

1865 The 13th Amendment of America's Constitution is adopted on this date in history. The amendment abolishes slavery in America and reads, "slavery nor involuntary servitude shall exist in the United States."

1869 The Colored National Labor Union has its first meeting. The union's purpose was to improve working conditions and the quality of life for its members and Black labor collectively and on a national level.

1932 Richard B Spikes receives the patent for the automotive gear shift for cars. His invention is welcomed by major car manufacturers.

1969 Ernie Davis becomes the first Black man to win the Heisman trophy. The award is given to the most outstanding college football player.

DECEMBER 7

1862 Fort Negley, a Civil War Landmark is built to defend Nashville from the Confederate Army. The Union Army forced Black laborers (free and slave) into labor battalions to complete the fort in the winter of 1862.

1863 The 62nd Regiment of U.S. Colored Troops is organized. They were a Black regiment in the Union Army during the civil war. The regiment was established at Benton Barracks in Saint Louis, Missouri.

1942 Businessman Reginald Lewis is born in Baltimore, Maryland. In 1989 he became President and CEO of Beatrice International Foods Company, the first billion-dollar African American owned company.

1955 Calvin Jones becomes the first Black college football player to win the Outland Trophy for best linebacker in America, and land the cover of the September 1954 Sports Illustrated magazine.

 # DECEMBER 8

1856 Harry Shepherd, African American photographer, is acknowledged on this date. Mr. Shepherd won the appointment of official photographer for the Afro-American exhibit at the Paris Exposition.

1919 Marian Saddler Taylor, African American cabaret singer, fund-raiser, and civil rights advocate, is born in Philadelphia, Pennsylvania. Later known as Marian Bruce Logan, she was a fund-raiser for Martin Luther King, Jr., Nelson Rockefeller, and Robert F. Kennedy.

1925 Henry "Hank" Thompson, Negro League Baseball

JAN
FEB
MAR
APR
MAY
JUN
JUL
AUG
SEP
OCT
NOV
DEC

JAN
FEB
MAR
APR
MAY
JUN
JUL
AUG
SEP
OCT
NOV
DEC

Player, is born in Oklahoma City, Oklahoma. Thompson is the first African American player to play in both the American and National Baseball Leagues.

1925 Actor, singer, and dancer Sammy Davis Jr. is born in Harlem, New York. He became one of the first mainstream African American performers.

1933, Flip Wilson, Comedian, is born in New Jersey City, N.J. Wilson became the first Black to have a National weekly prime time television show.

1976 The Mayme Clayton Library and Museum opens on this date. The museum is dedicated to sharing the stories of African American people in all its different variations. Dr. Clayton believed that children should know Black people have done great things.

1936 – NAACP files first suit to equalize salaries of Black and white teachers in Norfolk Virginia.

1987 Kurt Schmoke makes history as the first Black mayor of Baltimore, Maryland.

Statue of Bill Pickett in front of Cowtown Coliseum at the Fort Worth Stockyards in Texas

DECEMBER 9

1833 Lucrecia Mott establishes the Philadelphia Female Anti-Slavery Society to organize women in the cause of emancipation of enslaved Americans.

1890 Former slave and conductor on the Underground Railroad, John P. Parker is granted a patent for his soil pulverizer.

1919 Roy DeCarava, first Black photographer to be awarded a Guggenheim Fellowship, is born in Harlem, New York.

1922 Comedian John Elroy Sanford, also known as Redd Foxx, is born in St. Louis, Missouri. Foxx is best known for the lead role in the television show *Sanford and Son*.

1938 African American NFL player David "Deacon" Jones is born in Eatonville, Florida. In 2016 NFL created the Deacon Jones award for the most sacks each season.

1971 Bill Pickett becomes the first black person elected to the National Rodeo Cowboy Hall of Fame.

1976 Legendary NFL Player Tony Dorsett is awarded the Heisman Trophy as running back for the University of Pittsburgh.

DECEMBER 10

1805   White abolitionist and newspaper publisher, William Lloyd Garrison is born in Newburyport, Maine. Garrison published the *Liberator Newspaper*, which advocated for abolishing slavery.

1846   African American inventor and engineer, Norbert Rillieux, is granted a patent for his sugar evaporator. This process revolutionizes the sugar industry.

1854   African American hotelier, and businessman, Edward Berry, is born in Oberlin, Ohio. Berry owned and ran the most elegant hotel in Ohio at the time.

1941   Oscar winner Hattie McDaniel becomes the Chairwoman of the Hollywood Victory Committee's Negro Division.

1964   Dr. Martin Luther King Jr. receives the Nobel Peace Prize for his non-violent protests for civil rights for African Americans and other marginalized populations. He is the second African American to claim the honor.

1985   Actress Raven Symoné is born in Atlanta, Georgia. Raven-Symoné has won five NAACP Image Awards for Outstanding Performance by a Youth.

DECEMBER 11

1872 P.B.S. Pinchback makes history as the first African American governor of an American state, Louisiana.

1923 African American nationally syndicated cartoonist, Morrie Turner is born in Oakland, California. Turner was the creator of *Wee Pals*, the first American comic strip that included ethnically diverse characters.

1926 African American blues singer and composer Willie Mae "Big Mama" Thornton is born in Montgomery, Alabama. One of her most notable songs is "Ball and Chain" as sung by Janis Joplin.

1952 Spingarn High School in Washington, D. C. is dedicated.

Spingarn was the last public-school build in Washington, D. C. expressly for segregated African American students. It was added to the National Register of Historic Places in 2014.

1961 Langston Hughes musical *Black Nativity* opens Off-Broadway.

1967 African American comedian and actress, Mo'Nique is born in Woodlawn, Maryland. She received the Academy Award for Best Supporting Actress in the movie *Precious*.

1972 Yasiin Bey, also known as Mos Def, African American rapper, and actor is born in Brooklyn, New York.

Yasiin Bey, formerly Mos Def, performs with the Brooklyn philharmonic in 2011

 # DECEMBER 12

1892 Minnie Evans, African American artist, is born in Long Creek, North Carolina. A permanent exhibit is on display at the Saint John's Museum of art in Wilmington, North Carolina.

1899 Dr. George F. Grant, a dentist, inventor, and avid golfer receives the patent for a wooden golf tee.

1918 African American jazz singer Joe Williams is born in Cordele, Georgia. Williams sang with the bands of Lionel Hampton and Count Bassie.

1940 Six-time Grammy Award winning singer Dionne Warwick is born in Orange, New Jersey. Warwick has had 12 top-ten hits during her career.

1963 Medgar Wiley Evers is posthumously awarded the Spingarn Medal for his civil rights leadership.

1963 Kenya gains its independence from Great Britian.

1975 The National Association of Black Journalists (NABJ)

is established in Washington, D. C.

1995 Willie Brown makes history as the first African American mayor of San Francisco, California.

 DECEMBER 13

1903 African American civil rights activist Ella Baker is born in Norfolk, Virginia. Baker was instrumental in the formation of the civil rights group Student Nonviolent Coordinating Committee.

1923 Larry Doby, the first African American in baseball's American League, is born in Camden, South Carolina. Doby also was the first African American to play professional basketball

with the American Basketball League.

1942 Frequently called Canada's most famous baseball player, Black Canadian Ferguson Jenkins is born in Chatham, Ontario, Canada.

1944 First group of Black women complete officer training for the WAVES (Women's Auxiliary Volunteers for Emergency Service).

1945 Herman Cain, African American businessman and

one-time presidential candidate is born in Memphis, Tennessee.

 ## DECEMBER 14

1862 The XIX Union Army Corp, made up of mostly African Americans, is established in Louisiana and east Texas.

1917 Robbins, an incorporated suburb of Chicago of predominantly Black families, is established.

1920 Popular African American Bebop trumpeter Clark Terry is born in St. Louis, Missouri. Terry appeared on over 900 musical recordings.

1939 Ernie Davis, the first Black player to win the Heisman Trophy, is born in New Salem, Pennsylvania.

1945 African American journalist, author, and cultural critic of rap and hip-hop Stanley Crouch is born in Los Angeles, California.

1964 The decision in the case of Heart of Atlanta v. The United States upholds the Civil Rights Act of 1964, preventing all businesses of public accommodations to deny services based on race, religion, or national origin.

1968 Entertainer Sammy Davis, Jr. is awarded NAACP's Spingarn Medal.

DECEMBER 15

1865 George H. Woodson, African American Buffalo Soldier, lawyer, and politician, is born in Wytheville, Virginia

....

1883 William Hinton, developer of the Hinton Test for diagnosing syphilis, is born in Chicago, Illinois.

....

1933 White South African journalist and antiapartheid activist, Donald Woods is born in Transkei, South Africa.

....

1936 Writer of the dark and gritty life in the Detroit ghettos, Donald Goines is born in Detroit, Michigan

....

1949 The iconic jazz club Birdland opened in New York, New York with saxophonist Charlie "Yardbird" Parker as the first act.

....

1950 S. James Gates, Jr., is born in Tampa, Florida. Gates, an African American theoretical physicist, received the National Medal of Science from Pres. Barack Obama.

....

1959 The first African American woman to lead a presidential campaign, and political strategist, Donna Brazile, is born in New Orleans, Louisiana.

....

DECEMBER 16

1859   The last slave ship, the Clothilde, lands, bringing a shipment of enslaved people to Mobile Bay, Alabama

1961   The South African group uMkhonto we Sizwe (Spear of the Nation) is formed when nonviolent means of protest of apartheid fail.

1973   African American O.J. Simpson sets NFL Record for 2,003 rushing yards in one season

1976   President Jimmy Carter appoints African American Andrew Young as Ambassador and Chief US Delegate to the United Nations.

2000   Pres. George W. Bush appoints Colin Powell as the first African American Secretary of State.

2003   The bill to establish National Museum of African American History and Culture in Washington, D.C. is signed by Pres. George W. Bush.

2020   It is announced that the Negro League Baseball statistics and records will be integrated with the National Baseball League's, creating a single source for all professional baseball's data.

DECEMBER 17

1905 Nellie Stone Johnson, businesswoman, social activist, and the first publicly elected African American in Minneapolis, is born in Lakeville, Minnesota.

1910 African American jazz trumpeter and band leader Sy Oliver is born in Battle Creek, Michigan.

1927 Barbara Sizemore, the first African American woman to head a large, urban school district (Washington, D. C.) and author, is born in Chicago, Illinois.

1939 A member of the singing group the Temptations, and solo artist Eddie Kendricks is born in Union Springs, Alabama. Kendricks is best known hits are "Boogie Down," and "Keep on Truckin.'"

1962 Sherrilyn Ifill, lawyer, law professor, and a member of the NAACP Legal Defense Fund, is born in Barbados.

1991 Michael Jordan is named 1991 Sports Illustrated Sportsman of the Year.

2002 Robert Johnson, the founder of Black Entertainment Television (BET) becomes the first Black majority shareholder of a National Basketball Association franchise by buying the Charlotte Hornets.

JAN
FEB
MAR
APR
MAY
JUN
JUL
AUG
SEP
OCT
NOV

DECEMBER 18

1870 The first issue of *The Louisianian* is published by future African American Louisiana Governor P. B. S. Pinchback.

1917 Performing in such movies as, *Raisin in the Sun*, *Do the Right* Thing, and *Dr. Doolittle* (1998), as well as receiving an NAACP Image Award and a National Medal of Arts, the actor Ossie Davis is born in Cogdell, Georgia.

1944 In the of case Steele v. Louisville & N. R. the Supreme Court ruled that unions that exclude minorities could not prevent minorities from higher paying jobs because they are not union members.

1946 South African antiapartheid leader and activist Steve Biko is born in Tarkastad, South Africa.

1963 Ranking professional tennis player Lori McNeil is born in San Diego, California.

1970 Hardcore African American rapper Earl "DMX" Simmons is born in Mount Vernon, New York.

2007 Jacob Zuma is elected president of South Africa's ruling party, the African National Congress.

DECEMBER 19

1875 Carter G. Woodson, African American teacher, historian, and the person responsible for Black History Month, is born in Buckingham County, Virginia.

1899 Pastor Martin Luther King, Sr., father of Martin Luther King, Jr., is born in Stockbridge, Georgia.

1917 Journalistic photographer Rober McNeill is born in Washington, D. C. A book of his pictures chronicling African Americans at work called *The Negro in Virginia* was published in 1940.

1919 Hamilton Bradley becomes the first known African American Eagle Scout.

1924 The actress known for her portrayals of strong, dynamic African American women, Cicely Tyson is born in Harlem, New York. Her most recognizable works are *The Autobiography of Miss Jane Pittman* and *Sounder*.

1963 Zanzibar becomes independent from Great Britian.

1963 Best known for her role in the movie *Flashdance*, African American actress Jennifer Beals is born in Chicago, Illinois.

JAN
FEB
MAR
APR
MAY
JUN
JUL
AUG
SEP
OCT
NOV
DEC

DECEMBER 20

1847 The abolitionist and suffragist newspaper, The Pittsburgh Saturday Visitor, publishes its first issue.

1857 African American Episcopal priest and educator, James Russell is born a slave in Mecklenburg County, Virginia.

1863 African American classical pianist and advocate of the musical arts, Mamie Hilyer, is born in Washington, D. C.

1935 African American sociologist, Harvard professor, author, and recipient of the National Medal of Science, William Julius Wilson is born in Derry, Pennsylvania.

1959 Professional basketball player for the New York Knicks and community philanthropist, Trent Tucker, is born in Tarboro, North Carolina.

1981 *Dreamgirls*, the Broadway Musical about an African American girl-group from the 1960s, premiers at the Imperial Theater in New York.

DECEMBER 21

1816 Society for the Colonization of Free People of Color of America, later becoming the American Colonization Society, is formed to relocate freed slaves to the African country of Liberia.

1892 The predominately African American perish of Saint Perer Claver Catholic Church is established in St. Paul, Minnesota.

1911 Baseball Hall of Famer and Negro Baseball League player Josh Gibson is born in Buena Vista, Georgia. Gibson had a career batting average of .373.

1948 One of the world's top grossing actors, Samuel L. Jackson, is born in Washington, D. C. Jackson is most notably recognized as Nick Fury in the Marvel Cinematic Universe productions.

1959 Three-time gold-medalist in the 1984 Olympics, African American track and field athlete Florence Griffith Joiner, is born in Los Angeles, California.

1959 Duke Ellington receives the Spingarn Medal for his leadership and revolutionary contributions to the world of music.

1968 The first McDonalds owned by an African American is opened by Herman Petty in Chicago, Illinois.

DECEMBER 22

1883 Politician, and teacher, Arthur Mitchell is born in Lafayette, Alabama. In 1934 Mitchell became the first African American Democrat elected to Congress.

1905 James A. Porter, artist, and art historian is born in Baltimore, Maryland. Porter was the first African American art historian, helping to preserve the art and achievements of Black artists.

1943 W.E.B. Du Bois makes history as the first Black person elected to the National Institute of Arts and Letters.

1948 African American television and movie actress, Lynne Thigpen is born in Joliet, Illinois. Her most recognizable role was the "Chief" in *Where in the World is Carmen Sandiego?* and *Where in Time is Carmen Sandiego?"*

1960 Iconic artist who went from graffiti art to high art in his short life, Jean-Michel Basquiat is born in New York, New York.

2001 Shani Davis becomes the first African American speed skater to qualify for the national Olympic speed skating team.

JAN
FEB
MAR
APR
MAY
JUN
JUL
AUG
SEP
OCT
NOV

DEC

DECEMBER 23

1815 African American Minister to Liberia, and abolitionist, Henry Garnet is born in Kent County, Maryland. Garnet was a proponent of ex-slaves emigrating to Africa.

1867 Beauty and real estate entrepreneur Madam C.J. Walker (born Sarah Breedlove) is born in Delta, Louisiana. Walker is credited as being the first African American woman millionaire.

1883 Elder Watson Diggs, African American school principal, soldier, and author, is born in Hopkinsville, Kentucky.

1907 Afro-Venezuelan author, Juan Pablo Sojo is born in Curiepe, Venezuela. His books focused on the African cultural contributions to Venezuelan society.

1919 African American inventor Alice H. Parker receives a patent for a gas heating furnace. Her innovations are used in modern heating and air conditioning units today.

1935 Esther Jones Phillips, African American rhythm and blues singer of the popular song, "What a Difference a Day Makes", is born in Galveston, Texas.

JAN
FEB
MAR
APR
MAY
JUN
JUL
AUG
SEP
OCT
NOV
DEC

1832 The first hospital for African Americans, The Georgia Infirmary, in Savannah, receives its charter.

1895 The first African American to receive a doctorate in geology, Marguerite Thomas Williams, is born in Washington, D. C.

1942 Air Force Four-star General and administrator, Lloyd Newton, is born in Ridgeland, South Carolina. Newton was the first African American to be on the flying jet team the Thunderbirds.

1951 Libya is officially declared an independent nation from Italy.

1959 Film producer and director Lee Daniels is born in Philadelphia, Pennsylvania. Daniels has produced the significant African American films such as; *Monsters Ball*, *Precious*, and *The Butler*.

1991 African American inventor, Lonnie G. Johnson, and co-inventor Bruce D'Andrade receive a patent for the pump-action Super-Soaker® water gun.

1992 Alphonso Michael Epsy is named the first Black Secretary of Agriculture by Pres. Bill Clinton.

DECEMBER 25

1745 Saint George Boulogne, Black French composer and musician is born in the West Indies.

1840 John Henry Murphy, Sr., Union infantry Sargent, and newspaper publisher of the Afro-American, is born in Baltimore, Maryland.

1907 Flamboyant African American jazz singer, and band leader, Cab Calloway is born in Rochester, New York. His most recognizable song is "Hi-De-Ho."

1918 Muhammad Anwar al-Sadat, former President of Egypt, is born in Monufia, Sultanate of Egypt.

1959 African American Space Shuttle astronaut, Michael Anderson, is born in Plattsburgh, New York. Anderson was one of the seven astronauts who died when the Space Shuttle Columbia was destroyed upon reentry to earth on February 1, 2003.

 # DECEMBER 26

★★ The first day of Kwanzaa, Umoja, unity, is celebrated.

1894 African American educator and author of the seminal book *Cane*, Nathan Jean Toomer, is born in Washington, D. C.

1908 Professional boxer Jack Johnson becomes the first Black world heavyweight champion by knocking out Tommy Burns from Canada.

1915 Una Mae Carlisle, African American musical performer, is born in Xenia, Ohio. Her most famous performance was with Fats Waller

singing "I Can't Give You Anything but Love."

1924 Harmonica player DeFord Bailey, Sr. makes history as the first Black person to perform on the Grand Ole Opry in Nashville, Tennessee

1964 The first all-Black starting lineup in professional basketball makes history when the Boston Celtics paly the St. Louis Hawks.

 # DECEMBER 27

★★ The second day of Kwanzaa, Kujichaguli, self-determination, is celebrated.

1843 The first African American newspaper in Ohio, the *Palladium* of

Liberty, is established in Columbus, by David Jenkins.

1857 African American Congressman and educator, Henry Cheatham, is born in Henderson, North Carolina.

Levar Burton with John Amos and Ben Vereen at the 5th Annual TV Land Awards

JAN

FEB
MAR
APR
MAY
JUN
JUL
AUG
SEP
OCT
NOV

DEC

1892 Livingstone and Biddle Colleges play the first Black intercollegiate football game in North Carolina. Biddle won the game 5-0.

1939 Known for his roles in the TV show *Good Times* and the television mini-series *Roots* African American actor John Amos is born in Newark, New Jersey.

1958 Emory Tate, the highest ranking African American chess player of his day, is born in Chicago, Illinois

 # DECEMBER 28

★★ The third day of Kwaanzaa, Ujima, collective work and responsibility, is celebrated.

1810 Thomy Lafon, African American businessman and philanthropist is born in New Orleans, Louisiana. Lafon made many substantial contributions to numerous abolitionist societies.

1938 Sugar Chile Robinson, a child prodigy who taught himself to play the piano at 18 months old, is born in Detroit, Michigan. At seven years old he became the first African American to be invited to perform at the White House Correspondents' Association Dinner.

1954 One of the most honored actors of all time, Denzel Washington, is born in Mount Vernon, New York. Washington has won two Oscars, three Golden Globe Awards, a Tony and received the Presidential Medal of Freedom.

1978 Grammy award-winning singer John Legend is born in Springfield, Ohio. Legend's best-known song is "All of Me."

1983 NBA player Julius "Dr. J" Erving scores his 25,000th career point.

 # DECEMBER 29

★★ The fourth day of Kwanzaa, Ujamaa, cooperative economics, is celebrated.

1853 Inman Edward Page, one of the first two Blacks to graduate from Brown University, is born in Warrenton, Virginia.

1897 African American opera baritone singer with many illustrious opera groups around the world, Jules Bledsoe, is born in Waco, Texas.

1907 Economist and administrator, Robert Weaver, is born in Washington, D. C. Weaver worked in many capacities in the U. S. government, including the first African American to be appointed a presidential Cabinet member.

1910 Recipient of the Presidential Medal of Freedom for her involvement in civil and labor rights, white union organizer, Mildred McWilliams Jeffrey is born in Alton, Iowa.

1912 Lewis A. Jackson, African American pilot, teacher, and instructor of the famed Tuskegee Airmen is born in Angola, Indiana.

1917 Tom Bradley, the former five-term Mayor of Los Angeles, is born in Calvert, Texas. Bradley was the first elected African American city council member and mayor in Los Angels.

📑 DECEMBER 30

★★ The fifth day of Kwanzaa, Nia, purpose, is celebrated.

1919 Tuskegee Airman, intelligence officer, and mathematician, African American Theodore Lumpkin, is born in Los Angeles, California.

1928 African American guitarist, composer, and Rock 'n Roll pioneer, Bo Diddley is born in McComb, Mississippi.

JAN
FEB
MAR
APR
MAY
JUN
JUL
AUG
SEP
OCT
NOV
DEC

1943 The 555th Parachute Infantry Company, a company of African American paratroopers, is activated for service in Fort Benning, Georgia. The company was sent to the North American west coast to defend against Japanese Fu-Go balloon bombs.

1975 African Asian American golf icon Tiger Woods is born is born in Cypress, California. Woods was the youngest golfer to win a major golf tournament.

1984 Considered one of the greatest basketball players of all time, African American LeBron James, is born in Akron, Ohio. James holds the record for the most career points in NBA history, as of 2023.

2019 African American, Donzella Washington, graduates from Alabama A&M University with her bachelor's degree at 80-years-old.

DECEMBER 31

★★ The sixth day of Kwanzaa, Kuumba, creativity, is celebrated.

1884 Singer and actress, African American Georgette Harvey, is born in St. Louis, Missouri. Harvey had a long and varied career, including being cast as Maria in the original Broadway production of *Porgy and Bess*.

1905 Frank Marshall Davis, African American poet, is born in Arkansas City, Kansas.

1930 African American folk singer and composer, Odetta Holm, is born in Birmingham, Alabama. Odetta was known for her anthems of the Civil Rights Movement.

1948 African American singer Donna Summer, the Queen of Disco, is born in Boston, Massachusetts. Some of her most notable songs are, "Last Dance," "Hot Stuff," and "She Works Hard for the Money."

1953 Hulan Jack becomes the first elected official of African descent in Manhattan.

1952 Charles Ogletree lawyer, and Ivy-league professor is born in Merced, California. While at Harvard Ogletree taught both Barack and Michelle Obama.

JAN
FEB
MAR
APR
MAY
JUN
JUL
AUG
SEP
OCT
NOV
DEC

IMAGE CREDITS

SOURCES:

blackpast.org
aaregistry.org
blackhistory.today
history.com
blackthen.com
becauseofthemwecan.com

COMMON ABBREVIATIONS
USED IN THIS BOOK:

AME: African Methodist Episcopal Church
HBCU: Historically Black Colleges and Universities
NAACP: National Association for the Advancement
of Colored People
NCAA: National Collegiate Athletic Association
NFL: National Football League
SNCC: Student Nonviolent Coordinating Committee

**BUSHEL
& PECK
BOOKS**

ABOUT THE PUBLISHER

*B*ushel & Peck Books is a children's publishing house with a special mission. Through our Book-for-Book Promise™, we donate one book to kids in need for every book we sell. Our beautiful books are given to kids through schools, libraries, local neighborhoods, shelters, nonprofits, and also to many selfless organizations who are working hard to make a difference. So thank you for purchasing this book! Because of you, another book will find itself in the hands of a child who needs it most.

Printed in the United States
by Baker & Taylor Publisher Services